CATCH A TWINKLE

A FOREVERNESS OF LIFE IN VERSE

CATCH A TWINKLE

A FOREVERNESS OF LIFE IN VERSE

LINDA BAIRSTOW

Sunstone Press
Santa Fe

© 2025 by Linda Bairstow
All Rights Reserved
No part of this book may be reproduced in any form or by any electronic or mechanical means including information storage and retrieval systems without permission in writing from the publisher, except by a reviewer who may quote brief passages in a review.

Sunstone books may be purchased for educational, business, or sales promotional use. For information please write: Special Markets Department, Sunstone Press, P.O. Box 2321, Santa Fe, New Mexico 87504-2321.
Printed on acid-free paper

eBook: 978-1-63293-771-1

LIBRARY OF CONGRESS CATALOGING IN PUBLICATION DATA
(ON FILE)

WWW.SUNSTONEPRESS.COM
SUNSTONE PRESS / POST OFFICE BOX 2321 / SANTA FE, NM 87504-2321 / USA
(505) 988-4418

for
You as a Baby
now
Grown

AUTHOR'S NOTE

Dear Readers,

This year of verse was written with the intention of being read one per day—give or take—although of course please peruse whenever and however works best for you. I consider it my gift to you, to make use of however you like.

The opinions expressed are my own, and if you think you recognize someone you know in one of the flattering and positive pieces—then it might well be that person. If you think you recognize someone you know in one of the dishing, insulting pieces—then *oh no*, it's not them.

An interesting thing happened while writing this, when I got to around September or October. All along I had been trying to imagine who you were (...all those unknown "public" persons being privy to my personal thoughts), but then something began to crystallize. Even though I might not know you personally, or even your name, I somehow *feel* that I do. (Weird?) And not only that—*this is true*—(Corny?)—I love you.

Linda B

JANUARY

JANUARY 1

Hello!
Do we pick up where we left off—or did we leave off at all?
Or perhaps we meet for the first time-? If I once knew you, so sorry to have forgotten (if I *have*
    forgotten!)—but whichever, this marks a new beginning.
The sun shines!
It shines through clear panes of glass and through curtains drawn wide. It shines
Into this coming year's openness of our hearts.

JANUARY 2

It is easy to overlook nature's imperfections when they're covered with snow. As if any imperfections don't matter.
As if only beauty matters.
Crystalline, pure beauty. But is pure beauty a cold beauty?
What one sees looking out through the frosted window contrasts starkly with dry warmth and a clearly exposed room.
A room with visible imperfections. In the mode of nature—and *life?*—with visible imperfections.
Yet while standing in dry warmth and gazing out afar through the window, one can experience deep within
The contrasting, confounding beauty of existence.

JANUARY 3

Precise. Spherical. Tiny. Translucent.
Were they once wild roses?
One wonders—one wonders so much!—but must everything be instantly classified?
Their delicate beauty is here!
And perhaps that's what truly matters, and what underlies all else,
While the flowers from whence they harkened remain alluring, teasing figments of the
      imagination.
Wild suppositions of roses—run wild!
With the security of the beauty of—
Precise. Spherical. Tiny. Translucent berries.

JANUARY 4

When the fading moon glows defiantly in early daylight,
Holding anchor within its purloined realm,
Two mystiques overlap down here below. That of vague
Earthly shadows vying in corporeal displacement, while
Vague, hazy illusions vie
In slow dancing turns, twisting together and separating moonlight and daylight—
And time—
Into layers of lost enchantment.

JANUARY 5

Everything one needs to understand life can be found
In a song.
Every feeling one needs to know oneself is ensconced within
A song. One song.
Songs of beauty. Songs of determination.
Songs of joy. Songs of reconciliation.
Songs of love—and of loss.
You hear and feel and know the truth within because you recognize it. You've known it all along.

Songs of what you've yet to feel
And what you've yet to understand—
That's there too. Even though you've yet to experience it.
Songs still unsung—
Lying latent and beckoning within you.
Not real. Not yet. They lie—
Within longing.
They lie—
Lie simply and forever—
A song away.

JANUARY 6

Welcome the silence in your being when you—
Listen.
Experience a suspension of conscious thought.
An openness waiting to be filled with the thoughts of others. To know what is meant.
A *desire* to know what is meant.
Then you can—
Know.
Sometimes a person miles away can pick-up on what is meant.
Sometimes nonhuman animals can know. When they listen.

Rounded out when you yourself send out meanings into the open silence to others, so they too
        can be complicit in a vast communal—
Knowing.

JANUARY 7

Elephants listen.
They listen with their ears, for patterns of sound.
They listen through their feet, for patterns of vibration.
They listen for and catch intent.
They communicate with sound, with gestures, with... intent.
They listen for and relish understandings with friends.
They want humans to be friends, to be part of their elephantine understandings.
Within the vastness of silence,
Welcome elephants.
Elephants care. They are...
Listening.

JANUARY 8

Say you wake up happy, and look—there's a light! Your room remains dark, but over there—
    through a slit in the bathroom door—*a light!*
Your bedroom is feeling familiar and safe, but the light beckons. Into it will be will be… what?
    Refreshing water on your face. A relief of bladder pressure. A stretching of muscles to touch the door frame? A twisting—oh yes, twisting side-to-side. And… And… There will be something spur-of-the-moment and unthought of. Something surprising! and satisfying. Perhaps small, but something *only you* would think of. It will harmonize yourself, within yourself.
All you have to do is toss the covers back and explore that light.—
So you do! You enter, refresh yourself, and then…
Another light? Yes!
Your living room. You know you love your living room—with its further stimulation of thoughts,
    including thoughts of people, of things to be done, of new harmonies to be established…
But not quite sure what the new harmonies will be. Or the new thoughts. Stymied. Hopes.
    Doubts?
Dying for certitude but knowing you'll be taking a chance—to be smack inside that light—
But it's a chance you take, and there you are, experiencing your living room… But there's more!
    Lo!—with a flick of a switch the revelation of your kitchen. Which you enter!—enhancing your day further with kitchen thoughts. Now a new part of you.
You pull up the shades—perhaps squinting a little—a bright new day outside beckons. The entire world outside your home beckons. Are you ready for this? Why not? A new day, with all its possibilities, now illuminated. To enter into and make your own.
An increasing ascension of lights. *Into the light… Into the light…*
Forever into the light?

JANUARY 9

The skier readies himself atop the black diamond run. (There he is—up there!)
His goggles—pricey goggles—are snug in place. His designer outfit, no doubt comfortable and
    flexible. State-of-the-art skis and boots, maintained with precision.
Our skier has invested heavily, both monetarily and time wise, because skiing is important to
    him.
And his body? Don't get him started contemplating his body! We can assume it is sculpted,
    healthy, *awesome*.
And that body is ready! Knees flexed. Poles planted confidently for—
The push-off!—
Swooosh!
Agility merging with strength. Adrenaline rushing!
Icey sparks shooting aloft as he cuts a sharp curve next to the green circle run.
Ahh. A green circle run. A different sort of skiing experience for those enjoying the white, cold
    out-of-doors. Perhaps out honing their skills in order to advance to a more difficult run—
    or maybe simply enjoying the slower pace. Swishing on down in relaxed figure S's—
    meandering off through the trees!—singing songs to oneself. Adjusting the curves and
    straights to the passions of the music, when—
A poof of ice particles spattered in their direction! Like eating dust when a sports car races past
    —albeit more sparkly and pleasant—but still—
Were you being shown up? Was the flying skier feeling contempt for you?
Must one brace for more than one type of chill when bundling up for the slopes?

JANUARY 10

CHOCOLATE! Chocolate and coffee! Chocolate and port?
Chocolate covered eclairs. (*Yumm*...)
A dense and luscious chocolate mousse!
With whipped cream a-la-splendor. Not meant to be just sitting there!—trying out just a tiny bite...
How can something so stimulating melt into oneself (*ohh, ohhh*...) so smooth?
'Tis a wonder to bemuse.
To savor. *Ohh*—let's talk a lot!
Of this—
The truth of chocolate.

JANUARY 11

Somewhere yonder—adjust your vision to afar—and no, your vision isn't blurred. You are witnessing
Mists of the mountains, flowing and coalescing as if the wisp-strewn essence of a trance. Settling in valleys and nooks—drifting up—flowing back into themselves. Itself. Slow-*slooooow*-motion whirling.
And from within the trance—look in close—could those be (really?) birds rising from the mist?
Spirit birds.
They rise slowly and with certainty, circling, as if settling into our awareness that they are flying through more than one place simultaneously.
Leisurely comfortable in more than one place. Looping through each locale and pulling trailing shards of one location into and amongst the next...
While into and through multiple times.

Spirit birds.
How much would such a bird know? Would one know of human lives—and of *you?* Could they, with their pulling and weaving of time and space, alter one's memories—or feelings?
What about altering history? *Reality?*
Or might they be tying together loose ends? Helping all creatures make sense of a singularity.
Or (more likely) would they know not and care not?
Are these spirit birds merely creatures of a trance? One with the trance. With the mist.
Dissipating
With the mist.
Dissipated specters.

But... Does not a specter, by definition, once established, exist ever in one's imagination?
And are not imaginations something that is real?

Looping. Gracefully flowing.
Now, forever!
Spirit birds.

JANUARY 12

There is perversity in watching someone do something you would love to do, but don't dare attempt yourself.
For example, perhaps watching a cat stalk its prey (tail *twitch, twitch, twitch*) then—pounce! and rip it to shreds. (You would *never* do that. It is, however, what cats do. So imagining it is okay.)
Or perhaps taking secret delight in hearing others gossip. As long as *you're* not the one gossiping. (Although no harm in correcting a mistake here or there... Or helping the person say what you know they're trying to say... Or maybe, *just a little*, redirecting it to a juicy part...)
Or would watching someone primp in front of a mirror quality?—thinking it will make them look better than everyone else. Which it obviously won't. How smirky fun, however, to witness them standing in front of a mirror earnestly attempting it! What if it's even with pilfered grooming supplies?
For *someone else* to be immoral and selfish—making a fool of themselves in the process.
Jolly good show!-?

JANUARY 13

You are not a fool.
…Well, deep down you are not a fool. As soon as you know what being a fool entails, you stop
    doing it.
…Well, maybe you look away—just a smidgen—from seeing what being a fool is. There can
    be satisfaction living in defiance of it.
Well… okay… maybe sometimes you look away *a lot*.
That *would* make you a fool. But not necessarily the locked-in, bad kind of fool.
What you are is a human being worthy of respect.
I was a fool for over twenty years. The clueless, trusting kind. It only regarded one (albeit major)
    aspect of my life. Other aspects were coming along nicely. Honest, delightful moments
    were accumulating—
But not in the fool part. That part is a void which took space away from where longed-for
    positive moments could have been.
You want to live a life vibrant with positive moments! (Right?)
Flush with honesty. Getting it right. *Not* a fool.
And once you get a grip on visualizing what such a life would be like (this is what I, like many
    others have learned)—just envisioning a positive, vibrant life raises the odds of it—
Becoming what your life really is.

JANUARY 14

They are just too high. The clouds. And they take up too much sky.
The clouds.
Light strikes into them, enlivening pastel colors layered against shadows, which billow out and
    into patches of brightness.
One of my former colleagues, an artist, specializes in painting a seemingly endless variety of
    such skyscapes—and on the largest canvases (*gigantic!*) that can fit into his studio. But
    even then, somehow, I felt that *he* felt the canvases weren't large enough to capture the
    astonishment of how "too big" clouds are.
Yet here I sit, pen in hand, poised to offer you, via poetry—clouds.
Your imagination is my canvas—larger than any sky!—and still the challenge is daunting.
The difficulty lies not with your imagination, nor an artist's skills. It's the clouds themselves.
    Their free-forming contours. The absoluteness of their depth. Their *expansiveness*...
That fits insufficiently onto any canvas.
So I ask instead for you to picture *nothing*. Then let the blankness of your mind be filled to
    bursting with the impossible tease of clouds. Of that which passes off as mere clouds,
    but is—beyond us.

JANUARY 15

Too many flippies and floppies!
And splishies and splashies,
And gasping for air—*oops*—I mean gasping for *oxygen* from the water—
And doesn't that water feel silky and cool as you glide through it? *Ahhh...*
A flippy of fins, and off you go one way!
Another flippy and swishy—off in another direction! *Ahh!*
...But no—this isn't right—
Wait!—
What? Oopsy—*OOPSY!* This wasn't meant to be.
How could it happen? The Magic slipped and flipped right past us.
You *are* a fish.

(*Burble-burble-burble*-sorry. Didn't mean to turn you into a fish...)

JANUARY 16

Could there be anything more composed than a cat contentedly asleep?
In the sun.
Having found the perfect spot on a perfect day to
Bask...
In being a Cat.
Here! In its sunshine. *Ahh*, yes. *Ahh*, its warm fur.
The enthralling, complex, beguiling composition.
Of oneself.
One's perfect self!
One's *Cat* self.

JANUARY 17

Beautiful puppy dog eyes.
Ever seeing and reflecting your human
Soul. Everything that is
True and best within you.

Faithful to you. Your pup!—
Regarding their own soul to be as yours. Though surely
It was within them first—being
Ever true and loyal—but they
Never doubt it is you they are emulating.
Dog eyes. Dog Love.

JANUARY 18

A nose comes first. *Here it comes!* Gently whiffing, snuffling.
Ever-so tender and vulnerable a body part to be putting first.
But some things are more important. Such as—
"Is everything all right?"
"Are you, my person, going to be all right??"
Discerning the clues with such sensitivity. Such concern! Such bravery.
"*Is EVERYTHING* all right???"
"Yes? YES!—it is!"
With a woof and a snoof and a—
Well-soft sigh.

JANUARY 19

Whiteness. A ballad for you today of—whiteness.
To sing of purity!—Or of an absence? Of a blankness, waiting to be filled in.

Vast and blank... Vast and blank...
A vast and blank white world.
Void of shadows. Void of contrasts and shadings.
How to tell if anything is here? *Is something here?...*
Is something here?...
Void of heat... Void of heat...
White and cold. Cold.

Something IS here! Something IS here!
Everything is here! Unseen.
Unseen within vast whiteness.
Vast and white... Vast and white... Unseen,
Unseen within the vast and white. Unseen within white purity
Lies everything impure. All the twists and turns of nature.

Let there be white!
Let there be *LIGHT!* Let there be shadows and shades!
So hidden heats and unsung keeps
Within our lives cascade.

JANUARY 20

Mr. Snow Leopard, Esquire, Sir—what are your spots for?
If we may know.
How do they camouflage you in the snow?
Give you an edge on your prey.

Oh no! Pardon me! We don't question your skill.
We know you can outrun, capture and kill.
I see—yes, we see. We back off with a bow.
Your Highness's spots—every spot—is a *Wow!*

JANUARY 21

The world is tight. *Mmmm*, tight.
Inhale! It smells tawny, with teensy toes.
Exhale. Exhale *deeply! FEEL.*
The feel is of long-lost vistas.
Roadways of branches stretching out into the future...
Mmmm, yes. Feeling them.
Listen! Hear the tartness of fresh acorns.
Tasty, colorful sounds. *YES!*—sounds stretching out into
The inherent security.
The tightness.
Curling-up tighter. Tighter.
Warmer.

Inhale the loud, crisp thoughts of scampering—
Yes! Pulse quickening!
Adventures!

Hindsights. Restless, churning hindsights.
Warm urine. Fetid straw. Hunger...
The tightness. Closing in...
Squeezing...
Shivering. *Too tight.*
Will there *never* come a release?
An awakening? Fresh springtime and a stretching out, yawning—which feels so near...
So far.
Unreal.

Can dreaming be all there is to life?
Nothing, but a dream...

JANUARY 22

Barren tree branches cut sharply up into a pale winter sky. You can see them reaching up, up, from distant clustered patches.
Beyond the patches, far, *farther* hills roll silently with sweeping swaths of faded color. All held proprietarily within—
Distance.

A distance filled with—thoughts.
Those of humans and other sentient beings.
Thoughts suspended and gently tumbling about.
Do they merely hover or can they be sensed rolling along with the hills and swaths of color?—
Sweeping up and around open fields? Filtering themselves through the piercing barren branches.
Do they lose concentration and dissipate away? Perhaps to re-emerge into new formations.
New formations in new places—and in new times.
Ancient thoughts from seasons past that have re-emerged and are tumbling about in the here and now.
Within, and of, the—distance.

The kind of thoughts that linger and loll.
In time.

And all one can do, when inwardly silenced enough, is absorb these distances.
And wonder.
And wait.

JANUARY 23

It is all of your memories—an accumulation of your entire life—
And none of the memories. When you feel stale on an overcast winter's day walk.
Afflicted with an openness for more.
Each step along familiar, timeworn pavement in anticipation of—something new.
Bright, heady anticipation—oh, yes! But anticipation countered with
Equally desolate hopelessness.
Two opposing poignant emotions which are somehow cancelling the other out? Into your empty
    feeling.

Another empty step. Another empty step. Another. Continuing along the same-old pavement.
    Now frozen.
Listening! Keenly attuned listening.
...*Nothing*.
Bundled tight against the bleakness. Against—the nothing.

Another step... Another step...
Nary a bird, dipping down and alighting in a way never to be seen again, onto one of the leafless
    branches.
Branches stark in their emptiness.
Are birds now only a memory?
Are scurrying rabbits now nothing but memory?
A rabbit, please!
Or how about a flitting leaf? Just one! One solitary leaf flitting and bouncing across the
    pavement in an oh-so unpredictable manner. Something new!

...*Nothing*.

Will unique wonders ever come again?
Perhaps today is marking an end. One never can be sure when endings will be upon us.
What about your lifetime of memories?
Can those be enough? Why isn't it feeling like they're enough? Could the lack of experiencing
    newness be canceling out memories? Please *not-so* to all this cancelling out!

Another step... Another step...
Along the same-old same-old.

JANUARY 24

I gestate.
I know not what to dream.
I am,
But am not.
I have feelings, thoughts, sensations. It is real.
I care—but know not what about.
My reality and my dreams coalesce into
Me.
We are the same.
We are the universe.
We float together in darkness.

JANUARY 25

The jungle is alive with color, sounds, texture, smells, largenesses, smallnesses, shadows, light!,
      breathing things—plants, animals!—abrupt sudden things, slow things—
All a-jangle.
A jungle jangle.
Never knowing what will come next—but alert something new is imminent. Ever expectant.
Uncertainties.

Consistencies. The constant of heat. The constant of density, lushness. Humidity.
Known backdrops for—what's not known.
The quietude of suspense. Amid—
The jangle.
Amid the ever-present rhythms.
But never knowing when a rhythm will be broken.
Consistently inconsistent!
Jungle jangle.

JANUARY 26

Stellakarosma had a mighty fine life.
For a dinosaur.
Hefty and cumbersome, she could reach the highest branches of cycad plants
With a slow graceful ease,
And enjoyed her long, leisurely days.
Which came to an end.

Time passed.
Eons passed.
Many others of her kind came—and went. Countless mammals, reptiles, screeching birds,
    primitive life forms came...
And went.
We know not who they all were, but we know of them, and that somehow they are a part of us.
    Some vital connection! Yet all that remains for us to see and touch are... dry, unfeeling
    fossils.
Taunting reminders of something we know we should know. *But what?*
Something that's on the tip of our minds, as sometimes unrealized words lie unspoken on the tip
    of our tongues.
Something magnormous! Solid.
Solidly baiting our imagination.
Plodding through our lives.
Evoking the long ago.
The silence... of the long ago.

And Stellakarosma munches down a few more fronds.
She looks up...
And winks at us?

JANUARY 27

A toast!
To all the creatures yet to come.
Or can we assume there will be some?
With all new shapes and whatcha-will-call-its,
And thoughts to think, and places to frolic.
As yet unknown—
We only dream
The hallowed thoughts that hollow brings.
But they will know!
To them!

JANUARY 28

If you have wings, it is your way of being.
If you possess a human brain, that is your way of being.
Chimpanzee brains are remarkably similar,
But chimps don't have wings, don't sing songs—
Birds have wings and sing songs!—
Except of course those unfortunate birds who might lose a wing.
So their way of being is—a flightless bird.
Some humans have damaged brains. As such, a chimpanzee might cognate more complexly than an impaired-brained human. Or a human could be born that way? (Super-smart chimp vs. low I.Q. human.)
Each one, an individual! Each with their own unique way of existing.
Collectively we fly!—dig, fear, love, head toward light, swim, telepath, sneeze, dance, snuggle up, mate, eat, poop, detect, predict...

How to mark where one category of being leaves off, and each individual way of being fits in?
How to value the distinctions?

JANUARY 29

Hello!....ellooo....ellooo....elloooo....
How are you?....aryuuu....aryuuu....aryuuuu....
WHO are you?....aryuuu....aryuuu....aryuuuu....

The walls of the canyon are composed of rock. Are you talking to rock walls?
There are trees, bushes, flowers. Do you greet and engage them in—what? A shared
    commonality of nature?
What of wildlife—or any humans who may be present though out of sight? Insects??

Do you greet the air? An airless emptiness between canyon walls?
Or something *within* the emptiness? Spirits?—a god?—
In which case you'd be thinking something *was* there! Not empty.

What of time?
A conduit between times and the spaces? Do you call out into times past? Or lay an actuality for
    the future?
Perhaps calling out to your future self?

Whether into the past, present or future—calling decisively out from full lungs and a full soul—
    establishing your presence. Here! Now! Atop this cliff in this vast universe.
Saying—I AM!

Hello!....ellooo....ellooo....elloooo....

JANUARY 30

If the universe and all its processes are expanding outward
In time and space,
Might it not be expanding to and until—
A single point?
The point where it all began.
The Big Pifft.

JANUARY 31

First you bite into the skin of the smooth, rinsed orange, then wedge in your thumbnails to peel off the spongy wrapper. Mouth-watering anticipation! Now pulling the segments apart. Sometimes the process goes well. Or—sometimes the skin clings tight, segments uncooperative, withered. You may impatiently wonder if the bother is worth the reward.
An ordinary procedure.
Then, every so often out-of-the-blue—a forgotten surprise!—a bursting spray of the finest mist imaginable.
Effervescent!
Fresh!
Spritzy!
Then—

The spray is gone. Back to only thin air. But air that now, somehow, feels transformed. Perhaps you lean into it to breathe in any lingering, orangey freshness. But find no aroma—not really. Nor tingling, spritzy air. Not really. Yet the air vacated by the unexpected mist is *different*.
Something unordinary has happened within the ordinary.
And within the unordinary within the ordinary—perhaps a thought.
Maybe a thought that it is worthwhile to enjoy small things. Maybe a memory of past sprays-of-orange, and where you were and whom you were with. Maybe wondering about the science of it all. All sorts of possible thoughts!
THEN—

Within *those* thoughts—perhaps a realization that you are no longer impatient. You have slowed down. You are thinking and savoring. And within *that*—
Add this awareness: That there are depths within depths... within depths.

That there are effervescent sprays of wonder all around us.

FEBRUARY

FEBRUARY 1

The hat you're wearing—"simply feels right."
It becomes you and you become it, so there's no impetus to remember that it's up there, topping you off.
No one else seems to notice it, either.
Then someone says, "Too bad no-one's wearing a hat today. This would have been a perfect occasion for a hat."

The music on the radio while you're driving along perfectly matches your mood.
It becomes you—as if it "just *is*."
You reach down to turn the radio on, thinking this would be a good time for some music.

The life you're living feels like it *is* you. You've gone through some rough patches, which you consciously addressed, but now the sailing's smooth and you're comfortable with your life and yourself.
Yet... What might you be skipping over and missing out on here?

FEBRUARY 2

It's here!—or on its way soon! *Spring!*
...If you can find it.
A solitary crocus pushing its plump pointy head up through the snow, then opening wide its glossy face to the sun? (Not?)
A swelling bud on a cherry tree branch which bursts open, unfurling its beauty and fragrance? (Not?)
A wary groundhog, unsure whether to venture out into the day or take refuge back in the security of its den? (Not even today's fabled groundhog??)
But if such precursors don't herald Spring, then how to know?
Snow still lies thick in shaded furrows and lees—and odds are there is more snow yet to come.
Any solitary crocus, cherry blossom or prescient rodent could get a bitter comeuppance.
Yet don't you acknowledge and anticipate it? Spring! You *know* it exists!
But... When *will* it exist?

FEBRUARY 3

Catch a twinkle!
If you can.
Born of mischief?
See a plan—
Oooo, yes! A plan for setting right
Those teasing star lights—
Such tiny sparks of brightness.
That flare up with
Delightness!
For you to catch! And own!—And share.
Sparkling ideas! Where fullness is.
(Ooo! Ooo! Ooo! Ooo! Ooo!)
Let's twinkle!

FEBRUARY 4

Players on field. Kickoff! Ball's in the end zone! In play at the 25. Quarterback drops back— throws to the wide receiver!...

Fans know how to follow the plays and what it takes to score. (Right?) The rules are black and white.
And one knows that playing the game involves skill. Strategy. Cunning.
Some say that life itself is a game. It takes skill, strategy, cunning—
But oh!—not so black and white. So complex!
If life *is* a game, sports events are but one small component in the overall game of life. Games within games.
Much easier to focus on a single black and white one. And so energizing when following stratagems, assessing skills—and the thrill of taking chances! Each maneuver yet another calculated gamble.
Always with something at stake. In the sports events.

—In life?
In life, missteps and brazen risks can easily lead to *death*. All animals are engaged in what can be called this high-stakes free-for-all.
And if life itself is a game, who's to say what it takes to score? To "win"?
What would be the rewards of victory? Oh!—how much simpler to throw oneself into following an understandable football game.

I've got an idea! For now, let's only think about that. (Yes?) We will wrestle with life's complexities later on.

Penalty! Back to the 40. Passed downfield—INTERCEPTION!—Did you see that? What a catch by the safety! He's on the 50!... The 40!... What dodging! Looks like he's clear all the way—the 10!—YES!—TOUCHDOWN!

YAAAAAY! I win the bet! I don't? (No?) Yes, (hanging head) I don't. I know you won. Sorry. Got carried away.

FEBRUARY 5

Dangled from any steeples lately?
Not your thing? But if imagining doing so is fun—
And you spy a dangler, daringly done—
You could relate, and feel as one.
A kinship.
A thoughtful person, thinking ahead,
Spots that in others, and feels they're wed
Through common threads
Of spirit. *Let's hear it!*—
For likenesses, and feeling linked
With friends and family, those in sync
In pastimes, caution, daring, dreams.
Working, caring, laughter, schemes.
Coming through. Dancing! Singing!
Copping out. Losing.
Winning!
Feeling sad.
Ends. Beginnings.
Being lulled as a baby, submitting. Commanding.
Universal understanding.
Everything human.
And undercoat sanding.
...*Wait*. What? *Undercoat sanding??* Come again.

Ahem.
Feeling akin
With steeple dangling, learning, thriving.
Baby jangling, scuba diving.
Careless blunders, basket weaving.
Beholding wonders. Loving, grieving—*a-a-aand*—
Undercoat sanding!
In everything minor. Everything grand.
Everything human.
Feel the kinship??

FEBRUARY 6

The intrepid hunter-gatherer stalks the savannas of yore.
This leafy green? Not for consumption!—makes one convulse. But when dried and ground can
      work as a soothing poultice for wounds. *Hmmm*, yes, there's room here in the basket.
What about this prickly nettle? Yes! Its seeds are crunchy, tasty—energizing.
Over there—down by the creek bank. The prized red cha-koo bark is almost ready to peel off—
      but not today. Today I'm here for the sweet fleshy tubers, nalla-loo. Tonight's dinner!
      For alas, so many mouths to feed. Will I be able to collect enough nalla-loo? Chayappi
      will be especially pleased—she loves nalla-loo! Hope she's feeling better.
Will I be able to uproot them without mangling them this time? Much better if the skins remain
      intact. Special skill required. And my back hurts...
Yet pleasantries distract! The day's rhythms. Light that dances through the shrubbery. Serenely.
      Seductively. The low, mellow humming of—insects? No—see there! It's birds!
Sure would be satisfying to make note of this. A drawing? A song? To share. To remember.
And now—getting to ponder what may lie beyond. Around that bend—maybe a surprise of
      God's bright spherical chappa-loo!—randomly and happily spaced. (Just *maybe*...)
      But now that I've thought it, how can it be a surprise? But whatever surprise does
      await around that bend, it will include
Colors to appreciate, and patterns, and—can't stop thinking this!—wouldn't a bright juicy
      chappa-loo taste heavenly right now?
God has given us *endless* wonders to ponder and to appreciate! Events to look forward to!
      Dreams to come true!
Yet... The season and the world are not through with us yet. There's Chayappi's illness...
      There's my back... There's this ever-present underscoring of—
Uncertainty.

The intrepid modern-day grocery shopper stalks the aisles of the supermarket, hunting and gathering food and household supplies.
A-ha!—breakfast cereal! And such a large variety to chose from.
Toilet paper? Oh, yes.
And what have we here? Meat! And how thankful one doesn't have to slaughter the animal and package it oneself.
One doesn't have to do much of anything—except navigate this bounty.

And now—*behold!*—the produce department. A bonanza of fresh fruits and vegetables. All so compactly and neatly arranged.

One doesn't have to do much of anything—except take time, if feasible, to enjoy the experience. Giving thought to farmers who grew and harvested the produce. Middlemen who transported, processed and packaged it. One's market employees who stock it and assist us…
Enhanced even further when contemplating the role nature played, from whence the bounty originated—
And not losing sight of those for whom you hunt and gather! Which foods do they prefer? What is healthiest for them? What household items to select to ease and brighten their life?
A pleasure to entertain these thoughts!
But also—

One doesn't have to do much *EXCEPT* keep in mind the cost—and worrying about having to pay for it.
And wondering whether you're making the right choices.
And perhaps even weighing whether the farmers, farm laborers and middlemen are being treated fairly. Or whether you're doing your part to ensure there's enough food worldwide for everyone.
—Because one wants to have some control over the world they live in. To feel competent.
   Maybe you *aren't* competent.
Which can imbue the familiar chore with a haunting anguish of—
Uncertainty.

FEBRUARY 7

It can be hard getting up when it's still dark out. Are you wondering whether you have to? And it can be confusing.
Is it the beginning of a new day?—
Or a continuation of the night before? That seems right, it's *night*, yes?—dreams—*NO!* Must get up and begin tomorrow! So hard, though.
Starlit inertness. Shadows too dark, too deep. Bygone unsettling thoughts…
Cold water in the face!
Bright lights! Revving up the pace!
No good. Still hard.
Bodily deception can only be stretched so far.

FEBRUARY 8

The day dawns cloudlessly—clear and bright.
An atmospheric blankness.
The world is illuminated as clearly as you'll ever behold it. An empty canvas upon which this
    new day will be painted!
Will it be a good day?
It sometimes happens that one's spirits lift along with lifting of darkness, into a new day's clarity.
Clouds—come as they may—can be seen clearly. As interesting embellishments to the sky—
And embellishing the Earth beneath them, by way of ever-changing shadows. Ever-changing
    moods—
Which might be painted into your day.
As brush strokes keep coming!

Problems. Come as they may. Will you be able to see those clearly also?
Let's say... *Yes!*
And when you do—what you can see—well, what *can't* you see? What is there not to experience
    —to envision—to realize?
To *enjoy!* You would be having a good day. (Clearly.) So why not
Spin yourself around—*around!*—spreading your arms wide—taking it *ALL!* in. This presently
    cloudless, blank, bright! new day. Is *here! Is YOURS!*
Because you're primed to see it, and to engage with it—*YOU* will be the one to paint it in.

And because, as you presently hold yourself tight, having spun and welcomed and claimed your
    day, and as you breathe it in *deeeeply...*
So much of your painting will also, you realize—
Come as it may.

FEBRUARY 9

NO! You're saying—*IT'S MINE!* They can't take it away!
As you hold tight to something dear. A possession. A person.—
Your *LIFE*.
It is yours—*by rights*. Oh, so much so. *By rights!*
GO AWAY!
You're so NOT letting go. You can't. Relinquishing what is yours would be *Wrong*.
Although… Perhaps…
Some day, there *may* come a time to let go.
Some day, perhaps, a time to share.

Time enough to decide.
…While you have time.

FEBRUARY 10

Millions of billions of little creatures created tiny, lovely shells for themselves, attaching onto their neighbors' shells, then... perished,
Leaving behind ghost towns of intricate edifices.
Coral reefs
Colorfully splash the ocean,
As the ocean splashes them,
And while living creatures of the sea wend their way through the abandoned ghostly structures.
There!—a school of thin bright yellow-flecked fish glide serenely through a large central cavity.
To their left, a smaller school of tall striped black-and-orange fish flick and flash their way about.
Striped,
Like the ripples of light wavering down from the surface.
Striped,
Like the swaying sea grass, anchored in tight pockets of grit and decay.
Striped,
Like their shadows that lash and plait across the coral,
Deepening into the encroaching night—and into darker crevices below.
Wherein a furled octopus lies hiding,
Ensconced in total
Blackness.
And the tentacles of anemones drift, lit eerily from within.
And tiny fluorescent fish of blue and purple dart.
It is another world.
A world that seems to deepen into ever further depths—
Of timelessness.
...And a stingray cruises across the darkened sand, the edges of its flat, stealthy self rippling.

FEBRUARY 11

There they are—see!—right there at the end of you, in plain sight—yet all too often taken for granted. Toes. (Give a wiggle!)
Okay, maybe they're not important, not like the rest of you—save maybe our two big toes that aid in balance. But what purpose do all those extra little digits serve? (All those extra *cute* little digits...)
No functional purpose. Superfluous! Though maybe...
A reminder to not take oneself too seriously?—
To not take *anything* too seriously?
Cute, pudgy little jokes?-!
(Hee-hee-hee-hee-hee...)
And! Look down at the end of everyone else. *Every human is finished off with these silly things!*

FEBRUARY 12

Let your breath catch in shadows of birds.
When dozens of flicking angular shadows
Fleet across you,
Then suddenly—
Gone!
Dozens of sharp, angular catches of breath, as one single breath,
Rashly overlapping within itself,
Abruptly! cut still within you. Remaining swollen within you.
Then—
Gone swiftly with the shadows, with the birds—
Into more wild, surprising confluences of nature.

FEBRUARY 13

It is an illusion—it must be.
It seems so cliche. Such a precise order of colors: red—orange—yellow—green—blue—indigo—violet. Top to bottom.
Like a fantasy rainbow.
And its spectacular, sky-sweeping arc!—
Just like a rainbow.
And translucent! Each glowing molecule a-shimmer!
But *too* translucent? A translucence that vivifies into—transparency?
Into something that can't be seen? Not there.
Is its assurance of the sheerness of beauty and covenants ever *really* there?
But O.M.G.—Look up!—spanning wide across the heavens—
THERE it is!
...Just like a *real* rainbow.

FEBRUARY 14

I'm smiling just thinking of you, dear Sweetheart.
Not sure how to put pen to paper this morning, but you're a good one!—so however today's verse turns out, it should be a good one.
Not to use the term lightly. "Goodness" doesn't "just happen." You have had multiple set-backs and temptations, and you *made* being good happen.
It's heartwarming, and endearing, and you lay yourself on the line every time you trust in the sweetness and goodness of women.
Thankfully you've learned to be selective about which women to trust, as some would use you, but it's still taking a chance whenever you do—whenever you let yourself be vulnerable around us. Although being vulnerable has the plus side of feeling soothed and heartwarmed when you get the trust right.
As we (back to women!) can be soothed, heartwarmed—and elated—by you.
It's men who give you the hardest time, those who consider you a fool, which is an *OUTRAGE*.
You must endure them—and some are in positions of power.
Thank you for not giving in to their hype of male superiority and entitlements.
But here comes the twist. I personally think they are right—that men (particularly you!) *are* superior—but *never never never CAN A MAN SAY THAT!* It is a bias—B-I-A-S—and it is unacceptable for a person to be biased toward themself.
As women are out-of-line when they are biased toward themselves and go around saying *women* are superior. That is something for only those other than women to say!—when they believe it. Which you do.
So we have quite different takes on which gender is superior—and thank you, thank you, thank you for your biased opinion (which serves to counter-balance mine—so we end up in the middle, where we should be)—and you are multi-cool—and *fantastic*—and—*SMACK!* Happy Valentine's Day!

FEBRUARY 15

If life's a song
You are my rhyme,
And nature is the tune.
Scaling heights to Kingdom-come,
And howling at the moon.

If life's a song
Love sings along,
Our hearts beating in time
With every heart, a seismic part
Of harmony sublime.

FEBRUARY 16

Those who bring us music bring us kinship.
Belonging.
A belonging in life. In solace.
In all of existence.
In aligning our minds with universal patterns of understanding
Of things beyond our understanding.
Registering only the patterns.
The deepest, most basic of thoughts. In patterns.
Thoughts born of feelings.
Feelings born of thoughts.
Those who bring us music—
Allow us to yield into a trust of something vital, but beyond us.

FEBRUARY 17

Everything that loves has a soul.

FEBRUARY 18

It's ever green in the everglades,
With an ever entangling and bedangling
Of vines in mangrovian thickets.
...And swampy and galompy
With snakes and water fowl and swarming bugs,
And in order to make it through one must—
Snap to!

Alertness and skills being necessary because
Alligators sashay through the meandering, murky channels,
Ever hungry and on the lookout and if you're not on guard...
Snap!

Where knowledge and skills must take hold to see you through,
Lest an alligator—*snap!*
Can't be both! Will knowledge and skills snap in and win out—
Or the sashaying alli...
GOTCH YA!

(But what got-ya? The 'gator, or your skills snapping in??)

FEBRUARY 19

Winter Bleak upon the doorstep.
How to keep him out?
      He's full of huff and full of gruff.
      He's pounding! Rude! Outpouring!
A surly, burly force of might,
Stomping his boots and roaring.
(And he sure could use a shave.)

Maybe, come Spring, we'll let him in—
See what he has to say!—
      With huffy, puffy, wheezy fizzling.
      Surly power dripping, drizzling.
'Twill be tempting—but rude—to tease him.
Shall we let him sputt on our toasty toes?
A kindness? To appease him.

FEBRUARY 20

It's not just that the distant landscape is blanketed with pure, pristine snow—
Although that can be enough.
Or that each solitary tree or rock or blade of grass is hushed in white—
Although each can be enough.
It is when you love each distant landscape or a singled-out tree or a blade of grass, that the
    frosting of white becomes a superficial embellishment.
Enhancing that which is important.

It's not just that a lovely dress or spiffy suit is fashionably styled—
Although that can be enough.
It is when someone you love is wearing such a suit or dress that you realize what the outfit is
    for. Its full meaning.

It's not just that the world exists with all its wonders, singly or collectively.
It is when you love them that you know—
You simply *know*—
That each person and each being and each wide captivating landscape
Comes with its own intrinsic value.

And that each—or all—is enough.

FEBRUARY 21

This freezing *brrrr* of a day has the feel of snow.
As if at any moment fluffy little white flakes will start floating around and about.
Flakes born as the dense fog splinters apart into crystalline fluffs, leaving behind a vacated thinness.
Any moment now...
Exactly like a snowy day...
Except... Where's the snow? No snow.
Some special criterion, such as perhaps an insufficient moisture level, must not be being met.

The person's life has the feel of a good life.
The person has a pleasant-enough family, friends, plus an interesting career and hobbies—and enjoys engaging with them all.
Except... The person is not happy. Lonely.
Could some special criterion not be being met?
Who would know what was lacking? Would anyone care?

FEBRUARY 22

A quick guide on how to feel loved:

What you need to know is that as a child you deserved to be loved. Every child deserves this as a birthright! You started out innocent and good. Whatever provocations and turbulence you subsequently had to navigate, you were basically lovable.
If the nurturing adults in your life didn't see this and convey it to you, it is their fault. Not yours. *Did* you feel loved? If not, that's the snag, and it is now up to you to see it on your own.
First step: Stop giving your childhood caregivers so much power over you. If they screwed up, their problem. *Decide yourself* from whom you wish to draw.
Second step: No hurry! Take your time settling on a trustworthy person or persons—or maybe not even a person. You might conclude a dog deserves best to be listened to. Or a religion.—Or birds! What you are looking for is *truth*.
Once you feel it through your gut—that you are worthy of being loved, whether or not you receive it—then the pressure is off. You will have achieved fundamental security! This being the goal. (Fundamental security. Mark that.)
Once the pressure's off, you will feel it's okay for your current friends to love you, or love you not. They don't have to. You may love them, or love them not. You don't have to. You are each free! and entitled to your own feelings.
(Just be honest with yourself about what your feelings are!)

Third step: Also with the pressure off, you now can leisurely contemplate and decide unfettered which characteristics are lovable, and see if they're a good fit for you. Maybe in the past you felt bad about yourself for good reason—but maybe not. Keep honing yourself!

Someday a fellow human *might* love you. A dog or a horse—or a hamster—*might* love you. Or you might simply lie out on a fresh, inviting day and "listen" for the love of birds, bugs, and all of nature.

FEBRUARY 23

Nothing expands one's horizon, or one's heart, like being in love.
If you never much liked jigsaw puzzles, but someone you admire and adore finds satisfaction in assembling them, then henceforth you will think of jigsaw puzzles fondly. Feeling linked with that person when you do.
Your beloved may awaken you to distant lands and cultures, if they are integral to that person's identity. The cuisine they enjoy, their everyday life, their concerns, their holidays…
If a child you love—even an infant—perks up, bright eyed and bouncy to jazz music, whereas previously jazz "noise" had bothered you, you start seeing and appreciating its positive attributes,
Including the history of jazz, the instruments involved, others who enjoy jazz…
And all those who also enjoy jigsaw puzzles… Or softball… Or knitting… *Whatever*
It is the one you love loves!
Taking you on an exhilarating journey far beyond the boundaries of what you alone would have come to recognize or understand.
All this! becoming—part of you.

FEBRUARY 24

There are few who know the importance of and value adulthood more than toddlers.
To be responsible for one's own self! Speculation that both stimulates and boggles the mind!
    Coveting—*the rightness of it!*
To go where one wants! When one wants! *Doing* what one wants!
And *knowing* they will get it right! That the capacity lies within them.
Toddlers earnestly and eagerly champ at the bit.—
But *ooh, ooh*—NO IDEA of all it will take to get there.

With sympathy for these little ones.
Challenging as their behavior may be for their caretakers, they are darling in their resolution.
For we *do* want them to grow up—not settle into being helpless and dependent forever. They've
    got that right—so let's let them know we applaud their goal! We are with them, on their
    side, and have confidence they can achieve it. That one day they really, truly will
    be in charge of themselves,
But that it entails more than they know. As situations arise we can point out both the good
    aspects, and some of the difficulties of adulthood. Including the responsibility of it!
    Formulated as a challenge to be met...
Where their pride kicks in on meeting a challenge!
That of course *they*—incapable as they *presently* are—can do it!
And that their having to follow your rules and being dependent is *only temporary*. That you're
    sorry about that—as are they!—but that's just the way it is.
As *YOU*, firmly and consistently, lay down the rules.
No waffling, so no awareness on their part that you might be considering their complaint.
This is just the way it is.

FEBRUARY 25

It is curious how curious some people are. *What's inside that package? What's beyond that
 hedge? How did it get there?*
What will this field look like in 50 years? In 500 years?
Why is my friend mad at me?
Can that car make it up that hill? How long ago were cars invented?...
Invigorating themselves with speculation! A life pulled forward with formulating and exploring
 mysteries.
As each new answer, once discovered, fills gaps in an ever-out-of-reach understanding of...
 Everything.

It is certain that certain people are certain they know everything.
Everything they deem worth knowing.
When questions arise they're glowing! (Because they know they'll never be on the spot. They
 can always secretly Google anything not in their current repertoire...)
Just ask one for any information, then settle in for a long explanation.
So next time a know-it-all takes center stage, try asking for this information:
What is the difference between learning a multiplicity of facts and understanding something?
How much do you think you understand?
What is your criteria for things not worth knowing?

FEBRUARY 26

To someone I have wronged:
I made a mistake, and I am sorry.
I did the best I could, at the time, and still I hurt you.
So—obviously—the best I could do wasn't good enough.
Although you, in your generosity, trust my judgment—which makes it worse. Believing you deserved it!
So, since you trust my judgment, listen to what it is:
You did not deserve what I did.
I was wrong. I regret it.
(Oh shit, and all that.)
And do you know how to tell when someone is genuinely sorry—that they're not just saying it? It's when they never do it again. To anybody. (Especially not to you!)
They face the fact that more than willpower or good intentions are called for. They figure out—and implement!—what i*t really* takes to never repeat the behavior.
Then after time has passed and you have observed whether I have or have not repeated such an offense,
That is how you will find out if you are presently right in trusting me.

FEBRUARY 27

During a blackout, large swaths of the city are, well—black. Blacker than the night sky.
    Sometimes extensive suburbs go black...
Piquing one to wonder what is going on in all those lightless houses. Do they realize they've lost
    power? Are they suffering? Medical devices not functioning? Pipes freezing?
Imagining all those unknown occupants at a loss and struggling, do you find yourself inclined to
    maybe like and befriend them?
Now picture one or two people you already know, whom you dislike. If they're out there at the
    mercy of total darkness, might your antipathy toward them feel less important? Their
    qualities more apparent. Their shortcomings, well, just part of being human. Perhaps even
    —oh, golly—
Endearing?

And imagine all the youngsters and the young at heart in those swaths of black houses—with
    their candles and flashlights, huddling under blankets, telling ghost stories and *ooo-ing*
    and *aah-ing*.

In darkness—
A light of commonality. Of goodness.

FEBRUARY 28

When you imagine experiencing an activity, you sometimes don't have to actually do it. Or live
    it. You can
Live vicariously—
And learn the skill of furthering the imagined action to include its consequences. Then indulge in
    experiencing the emotions of that also! Then deciding which of those actions and their
    consequences you want to strive for in real life.
So... When ready! Settle in and get comfy to watch a move. Or read!—a story, newspapers,
    poetry, biographies...
Keeping abreast of the lives of public figures, in their assorted glories, defeats, trials,
    tribulations, jaw-dropping predicaments, multiplicity of scenarios...
Then evaluating where the characters went wrong.
And went right!
Most of which won't happen in your own life—especially science fiction scenarios.
And some of which would be dreadful if they did happen.
But you can imagine reacting *as if* the disasters happened—and maybe come up with ways to
    insert some of those satisfying thrills into your actual life, but by different means. Such as
    —*not really* sledding over a cliff, but taking a rollercoaster ride, and feeling yourself
    skyborne over distant valleys and rivers...
Or *not really* being a bad guy who sets up catastrophes.
Oh, no—*you!*—a good guy! One who helps keep life's disasters to a minimum.
By making sure the drama and possibilities that unfold on the big screen, and elsewhere
    vicariously—are enough.

FEBRUARY 29

A little extra sunshine
To brighten up your day.
Splashes of extra color
To paint emotions gay.

—*Oh yes!*

How 'bout an extra helping
Of chips—with wine and cheese?
Then slipping in a nap—and dreams!—
Outdoors in soothing breeze?

—*Why, yes, now that you mention it…*

Indulge in laid-aside hobbies!
Embracing love, sincere.
This vacant time to fill with truth
And and all that you hold dear.

—*Because you're feeling, why not?*

In other times, in other wheres,
There are lies. Horrors. Disease.
But not today, on this extra day—
Here's to you! At ease.

—*With all that is right.*

FEBRUARY 30

A nonexistent day.
(Pardon the intrusion.)
With experiences to be had, thoughts to be cultivated, understandings to be shared—
That don't fit in with time.

...Time, that is, as we know it.

MARCH

MARCH 1

Can one know a lion?
Really *know* a lion?
Is it only what a lion wants one to know?
Can you know when a lion approaches? Or in what manner a lion approaches?
Will it be with a roar?
Surely a lion wishes its intent kept secret. Behind any roar. Behind its glowing eyes, flattened
    ears—
With only stark leaps of our imagination to tell...
Until—as planned!—the lion wants us to know.

MARCH 2

The *pitter-pitter-pitter* of little mouse feet thrumming,
Stopping.
Go—
Stop!
What's it thinking? Why no blinking?
Off again
Staccato.
On again—the brakes!
Now whiskers whir, courage afore—it
Shoots for the sweepstakes!

We have a winner!

MARCH 3

Holding sway
In the inimitable way
That only a skunk can do.
      Partly alarming.
      Haute-ly disarming,
As it waddles on off. *Toodle-oo!*

MARCH 4

Sunlight pours in through gorgeously crafted stained-glass windows, splotching random colors across a darkened interior. You stand transfixed. As the colors glow about you, you feel—somehow—blessed,
As if the light streaking through the designs and depictions of the windows are transferring the spirit of the patterns through the light itself, onto all within. Onto—and *into*—you.

When light shines through leaves and flowers, one can be similarly mesmerized. You can sense the abstraction of the leaves and flowers—designs of nature—conveyed *within* the light shining through, as a blessing of nature.

Now envision a rabbit hopping into this scene, vibrating with life, all ears—delicate, veined, orangey-pink ears—which are struck through with this morning's light—
Bestowing blessings of delicacy, warmth—and *life!*—to all. To all who witness it—and all who *can imagine it*.
Blessings to all, through—bunny ears!

MARCH 5

Entangled New England blueberry roots cling tenaciously to what little sod they claim, forming small clumps of islands, floating above the earth.
—Yes, you read that right—*floating!* Up to a foot above slick, slimey earth. Clumps of blueberry roots!
What—I mean *why*—I mean HOW can this be??
As if no—*yes*—*of course* they are aloft—because there the islands are.
Right?
Or could it be that down-down-*down* into the obscurity of the dark moist crevices between them, that indiscernible tree roots—or maybe rocks?—are holding them up?
Rainwater might have eroded away layers of softer soil below the tightly tangled roots—creating an *illusion* of levitation.
...*OR* do you suppose—fantastically—eerily—that perhaps the blueberry islands *really are* floating?—
Distancing themselves from an Earth hell-bent on being realistic.

MARCH 6

It is not yet the vernal equinox. It doesn't have to be the vernal equinox.
It is not an exact waxing half moon. It doesn't have to be an exact half moon!
What it IS—*for us*—is the first day of Spring!
One's own body tells us when it's Spring.
Today my body is saying it is!
Perhaps yours is also?
Maybe your friends are thinking so too—for them.
My friends did, in that we all showed up wearing bright scarves or sparkling tees today for lunch. First time this year! Each of us, independently.
And all across town thermostats probably didn't need adjusting, neither up nor down. Ours didn't need to be.
Nor was it a fluke chance that the brightest scarf among us was a last minute affair? She had planned on a "tasteful" subdued one—but on the way out the door, enough of that. Enough of *Winter!*
Perhaps tomorrow we'll be back to lighting another fire, cloistered inside. That doesn't matter.—
TODAY something has happened. A corner turned. A serendipitous shifting
Within ourselves of hot and cold, bright and subdued, decision and indecision. Aware of what's behind us—bolstering us!—but no longer living it. *Looking ahead!*
A moment between differences, that takes into account all of the differences. Suspended within the—
Serendipity!

MARCH 7

Bloom! Bloom! Apache plume. Dot yourself with tiny white rosettes,
Tiny white kisses,
On a scraggy shrub that could use a kiss here and there.
In an airy flair!
Bloom!

MARCH 8

There must be a path to it... to something.
Something is surely in there.
It's a mystery.
One sees only dense, thorny shrubbery, splotched with dark shadows.
Is the something hidden within the dark shadows?
Are the dark shadows the something?
No—dark shadows aren't it. Our something is *substantial*.
The thick rugged tree trunks, then? Should we be satisfied with that answer and go home?
No, no. Something *alive* is here. Can't you feel it? Maybe if we're quiet it will make a noise.
    Shhh...

Waiting.
Waiting... Not breathing...

Yes!—*THERE!*
Did you see it??
One has the fleeting impression of a deer—a mule deer—kicking up her heels—but no. Only
A white rump? Exactly... *There,*

Where one still sees only deep entanglement. With insubstantial impressions, now lost.
Although...
Inhale! Might you be catching the delicate scent of freshly crushed twigs?

MARCH 9

We know you're a deer.
You are majestic, and beautiful,
And you're gracefully and attentively searching for water? Yes?
It's been a long, dry winter.
Bet you wouldn't mind finding a mate either—
And getting rid of some of those fleas and ticks might be nice.
Yes?? Maybe? We don't know,
And what we don't know, you do know. In dearness.
May you find whatever it is you're wanting!

MARCH 10

The lovely young heifer looks up to you with her soft brown eyes. Trusting eyes.
You have raised her since weaning—your young farmers project—
And soon it will be time for her to be auctioned off.
—For *slaughter*.
You can't do this. You *can't*. It violates something profoundly basic—something SACRED—
    within you.
Yet you were told—from the beginning you were *warned*—to not bond with the animal. You
    further knew your family could barely afford her, and the agreement was they'd be paid
    back post-auction. They consider the money necessary.
You are part of a farming community with many good, hardworking people. You value them
    personally, and what they stand for, and it's important to you to belong. *You value your*
    family! How could there be any doubt??

This was many years ago. I now have reason to wonder, looking back, if you knew how much I
    valued *you*. That I was on your side.

MARCH 11

It's not easy.

Growing up. Finding yourself in a position where you must choose between the lesser of two evils. Damned if you do. Damned if you don't. How can this be right?

And knowing whichever behavior you pick, you will be responsible for it. Or potentially worse—if you were to shrug off feeling responsible. For you now must pick between those alternatives, also—to take responsibility for your actions, or to place blame elsewhere.

Head in hands. What kind of a world is this??

You've long known adulthood is about being responsible for oneself. You loved that idea! Isn't that the glory of it? One's claim to pride! And you've always known yourself to be a good person. A moral person.

Such heaviness now. Could this be a comeuppance?

How to pull off staying moral and good?

And what about this newfound anger—rage!—at the *unfairness* of it?

MARCH 12

Those who bring us dance bring us
Delight
With what a body can do. Even if we ourselves are not the ones dancing.
As onlookers, we can imagine ourselves moving and feeling as the performer.
Feeling at home in our bodies—and in ourselves, our spiritual selves!—linking now with the
    rhythms!—Harmonies!—Melodies! Patterns. All one. Existence!—
All one.
Flowing between components, between dance steps—choreographed, freeform—emotions!—our
    bodies—
All one.

And can you imagine moving not just as a human body? Imagine yourself flapping, lifting up,
    twisting as a bird! Or—
Try watching an insect. See if you can you merge your sensations with its sensations. (Some kind
    of ditzy maneuvering going on!)
Grace and prowess when you're a feline. Athleticism and agility as an reptilian. Swishy in being
    a fishy...
DELIGHT!—
In all a body can do.

MARCH 13

Noses!
So twitchy, bewitchy, and somehow sublime.
So spot-on adorable. Snorable. Mine?
And thine—and theirs—up in airs they combine
Into sniffiness. Spiffyness,
Sweetly confined
In each small, tender pillow.

MARCH 14

Let go of her nose!
Can't someone stop you male sea otters from doing that?
Ouchie! Ouchie! And sometimes worse—way worse—as in a fatal injury.
And why? All because you want her to hold still so you can "procreate" with her.
Don't you like her? She's nice—*very nice*—and fun. *She's your friend!* And since you're nice,
 too—right?—then we have to assume you'd rather not cause her pain and injury.
As such, would you welcome the aid of human intervention?
Would you like us—on behalf of your species—to come up with an ecologically sound solution
 to this unfortunate situation?

MARCH 15

We have been put on notice.
A bird—*that* bird—is telling us so.
Right clearly we're on notice!—but not so clear about what it is.
Perhaps you can decipher its news:
Does it sound like we're being warned off?
Being declared victorious over?
Or maybe it's not talking to *us*? Are we inserting ourselves into some imperative bird-to-bird
    communication? (Eavesdropping.)
Or could the bird simply be expressing itself? A soliloquy!
Listen in close...
There's a definite series of trills, chirps, enunciations. Yet whatever its announcement, this can be
    said:
It is adding one small completeness to the universe.

MARCH 16

I surround you. You are asleep, yet I am here for you to know. I am everything—everywhere—around you. I am the night.
I am all the sounds you don't hear. Small, thunking flat sounds. Melodic sounds. Screeches and crashes. All present. Sounds that can be known without hearing.
I am all the sights you don't see. What might be pleasing sights. What might be harrowing sights. *All* the sights. Know that they are here. Within me.
Within you.
We are the night.
The life you will live in daylight, with all its joys, anticipations and challenges—is here.
Everything that *might* happen.
The life you have already lived—here.
All history, all activity, ensconced within me!
You—lying motionless—within me.
Within you.
The night.

MARCH 17

There once was a rat from Kildrakes
Who dreamt-up a thing we call snakes.
      They slithered unresting,
        His nest mates digesting.
Then tangled in tails he awakes.

(*Talk about a nightmare!*)

MARCH 18

Today is a good day to be a hero.
Let's say... That's you!
When an unfair or dastardly event is happening, then—*ta-da!* There you are, to save the day!
It's an attitude.
Some living being, somewhere, *will always* need help.
A stranded motorist, a woebegone student, a box of discarded kittens...
The attitude: Being alert to such situations, staying sharp, always a bit on edge.
Hero mode!
Scoping out the terrain, aware of your skills and limitations. Honing your skills. Honing when
      and how to apply them.
YOU!
Brave! Strong! Making the world a better place!
You are needed.
You might even (hopefully!) be appreciated.

MARCH 19

Follow that car! Off into the heart of adventure, setting matters right with your inordinate skills —intellect—bravery.
Follow that thought! Into the thick of more thoughts—such thrills!—solving problems and setting the world right with increasingly accurate information and insights.
Realizing when you crash—KAKK!—but with humility and determination, putting that car—your thoughts—back together, recalculating the situation…
Then off again! Back into hot pursuit!

MARCH 20

Who are the brave but those who couldn't live with themselves if they were not?

Who are the strong of faith—brave or otherwise—but those who through brute determination strive to do what is right?

MARCH 21

Sometimes it can feel as if the world owes you something.
Maybe just a kind word here and there. A hug. A savory, melty slice of pizza. A boat?
A victory.
Perhaps your sense of entitlement depends on how much you feel you've sacrificed along the way.
Having sacrificed your time perhaps, when you would rather have been doing something else.
Especially if your energy had been sapped. Or when your safety and health were being laid on the line.
Do you feel you are owed if you didn't feel you had a choice but to participate in such endeavors? A *fair choice*.
Because maybe you *did* choose, agreeing to what you thought were deals, but now suspect the other parties were manipulating you. Or you think they have reneged.
Maybe a boat for that? An apology?
And what—(brace yourself)—what if what you gave up along life's journey was your sense of self? Your soul.

Or could it be we're looking at this all wrong? Are asking the questions backwards.
Perhaps the starting question to ask is: What might you be *owing others*?
Then to go forward from there.

MARCH 22

Have you ever felt beside yourself?
Not knowing what to do.
As if you're standing there and another person is standing there beside you, trying to figure you out. (Another you.)
Each beside the other, and each flummoxed by the other, because *neither of you* knows what to do.
So this wouldn't be getting any better!
So you may as well get back inside yourself. (*Much better!*)
But are you back where you started? Or will have seeing yourself from outside yourself
Clarified yourself?

MARCH 23

The shadow flitting across the forest floor is a squirrel.
Bounding over amassed rivulets of pine needles,
Frisking around rocks and downed branches,
Body and bushy tail flowing among shards of light.

The squirrel flitting across the forest floor is a shadow.
Sun filtering through mottled pine trees.
Quick and random swishing of branches, casting down
A bushy tail, shifting embodiment—
And whimsical dashes of conjecture.

MARCH 24

Picture, if you will, a daddy-long-legs. With its long wispy legs, these spiders are often considered benign, goofy. Tickling a person's fancy.
Now picture the same spider, but with stubby uncoordinated legs, scrambling across your floor. Same little guy in his same core body—but creepy. Right?
The same can be said of beloved squirrels. Remove their extravagant tail and *presto!*—a rat.
And next (oh no...) puppy dogs. It is speculated they have evolved to have such soulful eyes and appealing expressions because humans favored these physical traits when breeding them. Over hundreds of generations, the pups who most appeared to adore us were those chosen to be replicated. A tiny-eyed expressionless dog, with few facial muscles, could have had the same adoration toward their human masters, but we liked it being obvious.
How much should one rely on quick first impressions?
How to calculate the intrinsic value of living beings?

MARCH 25

In softened time they float and furl,
Dancing with the air,
In graceful whorls above the Earth.
Above our countryside.
Taking our light—swoooshing it back—
In shadows far and wide.
Bowing in billowing pirouettes
To their partner, Air—
Who fumbles! Is unsated!
Wresting them apart in shreds.
Leaving, us all,
Vacated.

MARCH 26

Take one sheet of white paper. (*Check.*) Take one black colored pencil. (*Check.*) Take your ebullient! free imagination. (*Always available.*)
Wiggle your fingers around in circular motions. Churn your arms—body—legs in circular motions. Think—*CIRCLE*.
Time to begin! Put pencil to paper and draw in the lower center—one medium circle.
Atop that—one smaller circle. Atop *that*—two smaller-yet circles (ears).
(Cute ears.)
For the face, draw in two round eyes. Wide-open, winsome eyes. Embellish, as strikes your fancy, with lashes, pupils—perhaps leaving a triangle of white in each pupil as a reflection of light
Next add a round snout, then a small solid black (round) nose inside it, toward the top.
On-side the body, two chubby arms, then paws, palms, fingers (all round)—(of course!).
Two identical circles next to each other inside the body circle, on top of its bottom line. These are legs sticking straight out toward us, so they are seen only as circles. With circle feet inside them. Then toes.
(Wiggle your own fingers some more, whenever they start feeling cramped. A final breath. He's almost here!)
He sure could use a belly. So—add another circle, centered in the body—leaving it blank inside. Empty. Think—*bamboo shoots!* Tender bamboo leaves. Hidden inside—having been munched and swallowed down into your...?
Wait! Not yet. Not before a finishing boldness.
Color in solid black between belly circle and body circle.
More solid black elsewhere—*anywhere*—as befits a... a...
As befits your handsome, satiated (with all that bamboo!) all-aroundy, astoundy...
What??

MARCH 27

Up there, my hungry friend—look what we have here!
A vulnerable, plump mammalian morsel,
Hung neatly from a tree by its own tail.

Hmm... Pinky and soft,
With an oh-so-possummy nose and whiskers,
And outstretched claws

Which catch the ground as it plops down.
But this is no good.
Look—it's dead.
Let's pay no attention to him.

MARCH 28

Silken curves of cactus seamlessly glide
Into their own dark crevices. Re-emerging—
With glowing triumph!—into
Swollen discs of terre verte,
Streaked with crisp black shadows of clustered spikes.
Having absorbed moonlight deep within.

MARCH 29

We have planted seeds. But will they grow??
We have cultivated the earth, toiling, and are now committed to tending the emerging crop until harvest.
Committed. Must stay put. Cannot leave, however strong the lure of our former nomadic life.
Committed.
Whose idea was this? Wise old women who wanted to ensure health and stability for our families? Wise old men, who listened to wise old women?
Those who liked our emerging culture, and wanted to anchor it in for personal profit?
Or was it decreed by the gods? That would solve that. Blame the gods! *Thank* the gods? Worship and prostrate oneself before the gods, in whose jurisdiction it is tempting to believe the fate of all resides.
Well, what's done is done. The seeds are planted.
Will they grow? Shall we appeal to the gods for a thriving crop? ...And woe to those who don't show gratitude to them if, a thriving crop it is. Wrath of gods!
But—wrath on *US?* Why not wrath on our enemies? Why wrath *at all?*
Doubt all that will make much difference to the seeds.
Where do gods, or a single god, fit into life, anyway?

MARCH 30

The farmer laments having to till the soil yet again, and again ready his machinery and schedule for the new season.
Not that the farmer doesn't value being tied directly to the earth and with life cycles of growth.
So why the sorrow?

The farmer laments that farming is not like it used to be. That one now must use noxious pesticides and fertilizers in order to compete and turn a profit. To keep the produce coming.
Not that he doesn't value his vital link in feeding the world's populace. That he's doing his part.
So why the sorrow?

The farmer laments having to make decisions that don't seem to matter. Too much is already decided for him. Including what crops to plant, how to tend them, and machinery availability and maintenance. Especially machinery maintenance! This farmer's personal expertise!—and pride. Now tractors and combines come with pre-programed computerization in sealed up compartments. (Isn't that going too far?) He can no longer diagnose and fix one when it breaks down! Must wait for days—sometimes weeks, holding up operations.
And oh, it adds so much to expenses.
Not that he doesn't value owning and running his own business. Some measure of independence there! Moreso than most folks, he's aware. And he knows he's contributing to the well-being of his family—and by doing honest, down-to-earth, sweaty, physically satisfying labor. He can hold his head high!

So why the anguished weariness?
A heaviness. A sorrow.

MARCH 31

To know a lamb
Is to love a lamb.
But not because of its characteristic gentle eyes, appealing soft fleece, trusting disposition.
To know a lamb is to know it as an individual—its personality, its quirks, and how it alone
    interacts with life.
Each lamb thinking for itself, making its own decisions. Coming and going as *it* decides, having
    assessed the available options.
It's not for any of us to assume ownership of its decisions! Its soul. Banish feelings of such
    ownership!
Embrace—
Love for *each* lamb.

APRIL

APRIL 1

(Alas.) It is April Fools' Day. Several ways to go with this. Wondering if maybe we should celebrate the fools among us? Yet at some point in our lives, each of us has been a fool. (Right?) Or will be. Should this be a day to acknowledge that part of being human—toward being a good sport about it?—*laughing* about it?
Happy—"How Fun to Be a Fool Day!"-?
That doesn't sit right.
Isn't it more enjoyable to watch someone else being a fool than to intentionally let yourself be one? So how about—setting up others for it? Playing jokes on them?
At some point laughing comes into it.
And being a good sport.
And well, yes—maybe getting even with people. When you hold a grudge against someone (small grudges, let's say), with a gleaming urge to set matters right? In an acceptable way. So you can go back to liking whomever it is.
Balancing the scoreboard.
No telling, though, if your notion of balancing the scoreboard and their notion of balancing the scoreboard will be the same. One or the other of you is sure to come out ahead. Depending how exacting you each are.
But maybe, after all, might not being able to keep exact score be the point? To be a good sport *about that*. That we are all in this life together, and we all become a fool at times and are sometimes in positions to hold grudges—for some people do deserve to be gotten even with—but sometimes that's sure to be you—and keeping tabs and scores can get all messed up. Too complex to agree on.—
So that's something that could be laughed about!
And to trust your friends are in on the mutual laughing, this one day a year.
Happy—"All of Us Going Ahead and Teasing and Playing Jokes on Each Other Day!"

APRIL 2

How to explain humor to someone who doesn't get it? Well, horses understand humor. So—
 introduce them to a horse. For the horse to explain!
A formal introduction—and preferably to a well-loved happy horse. (But any horse will do.)
The formal introduction being part of the joke. And to be absolutely serious about it—"the
 telepathic horse." *Sincerely* serious. For a horse is a sincere being, to be respected.
The clueless human must recognize the horse's sincerity. Then leave them alone together to
 ponder one another—
And let the ridiculousness of their predicament dawn on them.
Humor? Wait for our human to be in on it!

APRIL 3

To an adversary:
I will smile if you will.
I know we disagree on issues—some serious indeed—but there is one thing we *can* agree on:
    That we are both well-meaning, good individuals, who want what's fair and best for everyone. Right? However much we may have different opinions on what that is.
We are in agreement on that?? (You've said—yes.)
Which begs the question:
Does your notion of what's fair for everyone entail you deserving better treatment than those you consider beneath you?
Such as, say—those who don't share your opinions?
Hey, I'm standing right here. That's *me*.
But our premise is that we are equally good, well-meaning people—which is how I am thinking of you right now—and how you are thinking of me...
Right?

Cracking a smile yet?
(I'll even go first...)

APRIL 4

I am not here to pass judgment on you.
I am here to understand.

Put a gavel in my hand, and I will judge you on the issue under consideration. Give me authority over you in any capacity, and I will make decisions. Whatever I conclude is best.
So allow me—and help me please—to figure you out.
Because before acting—and before understanding—
Your totality as a person is what's important.
You come first.

APRIL 5

Chloro-phyll-a-filled slivers of green
Reach up...
Piercing the air with tiny shrieks
Of determination.
Reaching up... up... up...
Toward sunlight. Toward destiny.
Toward becoming a new meadow!
(*shriek!... shriek!... shriek!...*)
UUUP...
To lay out a fresh new patch of the world.

...And to tickle the tummies of coyotes.

APRIL 6

A spot on a ladybug is—
Spot on!
As are spots on leaves? On feathers?
So self-contained, perfect, concise, unassuming.
Dottings of fun—*dit!-dit!-dit!*—an attuning,
Each striking a precise spot in one's mind.

APRIL 7

Windy days, blowing, blowing.
Gentle, forceful, mighty, flowing.
To confront its verve, feel the oncoming force—
Gushing, swirling wind!—
Tousling your hair, cooling your skin,
Daring your soul to think in its course.
(Do you dare?)
To—align your gaze with
      Its swirls and careen-ery!—
      Whipping free and brash throughout the scenery.
Owning deep its carefree ways.

Windy days! Blowing, blowing.
Gentle, forceful, mighty. Flowing.

APRIL 8

Rain talks. It sings. It dances! In merry traipsing, virtuoso shimmies, gutsy reeling. Splashing—
      s*inging!* Sputtering—*talking!*— on... and on... in arrhythmic rhythms.
...Settling into a
Prattling mode.
Is the rain—could it be?—*telling stories?* Oh, the stories rain could tell!
How to know? How to listen??
A-hush. In the quiet of one's mind. In the consonant prattle of the rain—
With the accompaniment of rattling windows, thrumming leaves, dripping roofs.
Hush. *Are* they there? The stories rain is telling.

APRIL 9

Having started out as a gentle rain—but then a vehement battering!—has scoured layers of grime
    from the city's cramped juxtaposition of skyscrapers, storefronts, alleyways...
And has cleansed the air itself. Now clear, fresh. But *dark*—
The late, late, dark, dark morning of a looming day
On a neglected side street.
The darkness pierced with a scattering of lights. Bright streaks of crisp color, fading out into the Night—
And mirrored on the wet pavement. The long streaking lights.
Within the quiet. A quiet that echoes sullenly up from the wet puddled pavement.
The reflected, doubled streaking lights.
The amplified—quietude.
This late night city tableau. Scrubbed clean. Lying...
In wait.
A distant car rumbles, vibrating the pavement.
Reflections waver. Distort.
Settle.

APRIL 10

Have you ever had someone forgive you for something you didn't do—
And something you would *never* have done?
Such as, say, kick an ailing, faithful dog of a friend when the friend wasn't looking?
But the dog yelps and the vet diagnoses bruised ribs—and your friend, in his anger and confusion believes—actually *believes*—you kicked her. (No other explanation being available.)
Then when you deny it, he accuses you of *being a liar,* to boot. How could he think that of your character??
What to do?
What your "friend" does is agonize and finally finds it in his heart to forgive you. (You each do miss one another.) But now, in addition to his base insult to you, he thinks he's being the better person! And... if you don't accept his generous offer of forgiveness, that would make you even less of a lesser.
But—*you didn't kick the dog!*

Another question: Imagine the religion of your culture would have you believe that deep-down you are a bad person. That as a human, you are born that way. In this situation, if left to your own devices, would you act out being bad?

But you are not basically bad! Or evil. Humans are in fact born—as are most mammals—basically loving.
Would you feel in need of, and accept, forgiveness for being fundamentally bad?

APRIL 11

(More *questions*.)

Does intending to do something good count if the person doesn't do it?

Meet "Sherilyn", breezy, intelligent, who has used her intelligence to figure out exactly what the most supreme, wonderful woman would do in any situation. And how to be convincing that whatever that is—that's her!

Even though her follow-through is abysmal. Yet as long as she *meant* well, she feels entitled to the accolades and rewards of having followed through.

The rest of us are supposed to forgive her, because her excuses sound so valid. (Something else she's adept at!) Further, Sherilyn enjoys making others feel inferior if they don't go along with forgiving her—*her*—such a sincere, well-intentioned person. (As in, good people are supposed to forgive.)

Would *you* forgive Sherilyn if she, for example, caused a project of yours to fail when she had "better" things to do than her part, as promised? Or when she balks at repaying a loan? (Among friends, she says, one only has to *intend to*. That we know she would if she could.)

How would you feel if others let her off the hook for a wrong she did *to you?*

APRIL 12

Do hummingbirds live faster than everyone else?
Whirr-whirrrrr-whir!-whizzzzzz.
Or does time seem perfectly ample to them,
While the rest of us seem to be moving very slo-oo-owly?

Do tortoises race along in their minds?
While the rest of life whips by even faster?
Diligently balancing home and ambition,
Then tucking in to settle the flurry.

Do each and do all, on land and in air,
Speed up or slow down, apace with their cares?
Venturing forth—every here, every there.
To the rhythmic beat of their heart.

APRIL 13

Feel the beat, the rhythmic beat.
Reach out and match it with your feet.
Giraffes reach far, necks sway, catch up.
Repeat. Repeat. Repeat.

Short legs will ofttimes mince their steps,
A shifting, shuffling cadence kept.
Repeat. Repeat. Repeat.

Lithe backs arch up as their hind feet
Thrust out between far stretched front feet.
Repeat. Repeat. Repeat.

Now rushing gaits!
And breaths varooming,
With pumping hearts, *papoom, papooming*.
Animating health.
As health goes on... And on...
And on.

APRIL 14

Clump-clop. Clump-clop. Clump-clop.
Sturdy little Burrito trudges on,
In harmony with his inner secret musings.
Taking life
A-pace.
There is much going on in life to muse about!—but it can't be done too fast—too hyper.
    Wouldn't fall into place right. Must go—right-left, right-left, right-left.
Since colt-hood, this successful pattern wired in. Not to be messed with!
Clump-clop. Clump-clop. Clump-clop.
Who is this with me? Why, that's my best buddy, Lisa!
She understands the pattern, but not the necessity of pausing now-and-again for a little nibble.
    Lisa needs to learn this. Must teach her, but she can be so—*stubborn!* It's one of life's
    enigmas worth musing about.
Clump-clop. Clump-clop. Sometimes maybe a little faster. Sometimes slower.
Marking time—and *making* time. Time where everything fits in. The daily routines. Being fed.
    Groomed. Settling in with my own dramas. All—
A-pace. (*Ha! Got a nibble in!*)

APRIL 15

When acute loneliness
Collides with an acute, compacted sense of everything—
Does that person's heart stop beating?
Would they just up and—
Die?

Or—
If one were to face such a collision, would it prove stimulating?
There would be truth in it. Truth in loneliness.
And truth in bravery. The bravery of facing such a calamity.
And in allowing oneself to feel the august sense of—*EVERYTHING*. (But, oh heavens!—To feel
  it *compacted*. All compressed together, *at once*.)
Creating the paradox:
When one does see it—and feel it—*EVERYTHING*—then they instantly *would know* they are not
  alone. Their loneliness should dissipate—*poof!*—in the moment of impact. Annihilating
  the impact.

Looked at another way, to feel you are part-and-parcel of this vast multiverse, you must
  recognize you.are alone. Starkly alone—within yourself. Trapped. *So then—*
You are positioned to look about and see everyone else trapped also. So many of you in the same
  situation. Not alone!
And all you need do is reach out to *just one* of them, human or non, to experience a personal
  connection.
And from that initial connection to go forth spacing out and pacing your lives together.
Easing apart the frightful compaction.

APRIL 16

Did you know that bobcats wag their tails? I hadn't known that.
But right here—*now!*—just outside my side window—three bobcat kittens playing, *and*—
    they're *wagging their tails!* For sure!
Bobcats have stubby tails (as you may have known), but not short stubs. They're rather long
    stubs. And when excited, they wag them, much the same as dogs do—
At least these ones are. (See!) All three kittens, frisking—circling around one another, crouching
    —pouncing!—*Oh, the thrill!* Rapid-fire wags!
My friends, enamored as they are of bobcats, will love hearing about this! Can't wait to tell
    them. For sure!
Except... Come to think of it... Maybe these aren't really kittens any more. *Two years ago* they
    were kittens, and they are certainly *behaving like kittens,* but...
Much larger, and what claws they must have now. And teeth. And—*strength*. Full-size, full-
    strength bobcats. On their own. Should they still be playing like this?
They each look around sharply, expectantly, for something to attack. Butterflies? Yes! A blowing
    flower head? Yes!
Cute? *Umm...*
Time for me to walk down the drive to fetch this morning's paper. Can't help but draw their eye.
    Was just on my way out—confidently—to fetch it. *Umm. Ummmm...*
Perhaps it's time to stop being *so sure* about things...

APRIL 17

Neck-a-neckin',
Peck-a-peckin',
Dapper topknots regale.
Hob-a-nobbin',
Dithered mobbin'—
Whither
Go the quail.

APRIL 18

When big sisters fall in love
Entire households can get turned topsy-turvy—
A-buzz with excitement!
Anticipation!
> When will he call next?
> *Will* he call??
> Will he keep being delighted with her ideas?...
> Where should they go out next?...
> What outfit should she wear?...
> Will he (*gasp!*)—*Propose?*

The adults can be in on the excitement also—although one is unsure why *they* are excited. Do they see the *real reason* your big sister is in such a tizzy?
You get it!
There is someone in the world—besides yourself—who sees all her qualities. Who sees her as her optimized self. Her *true* self—flush with her competence, and all that she can be. As if that's *already* her.
After she's lived with debilitating uncertainty about her herself and her future—to have a man in the picture—*for real*. And maybe he's sure enough of what he's seeing to be willing to take a chance on her!
(How can the adults be in on that? It's not like they ever thought her ideas were so delightful, so fun. Are they mostly thrilled at the prospect of having her out of the house?)
And get ready for the best *bestest* part—
It's the reciprocity! It's that Big Sis is seeing *her boyfriend's* optimized self. They are seeing each other through each other's eyes! (How romantic is *that?*) And she's right, too—you also can see his optimized self.

But, okay. There *IS* something else going on... Something maybe to jinx it. Something—well—untrue?—about this.

It somehow feels like—*a fantasy?*

Your sister gets what's going on. Her boyfriend gets it. You know this. It's *you* who's missing something.

It's as if... there's too much reality in the way.

Reality you don't understand yet. Futures—and responsibilities?—that are smack there in front of you that you are unable to fathom.

And where does sexuality come into it? How big of a deal is sex?

But mostly—how could anyone ever see in you the qualities and profound wonder that your sister's boyfriend is seeing in her?

Nonetheless... Here, now, palpable exhilaration is reverberating among *ALL* of you!

But... Where do you fit in? Though *maybe*...

Maybe someday, when you're older... someday when you've grown and understand more... then (*gasp!*)—

Could there come a time, in your life, when *you too* will be in on love's secrets??

APRIL 19

A fresher, brighter, more promising day—there never was!
You shuffle the order of your assignments, rushing through them and wresting open a mid-morning break. This is a day meant to be *outside*.
Blossoming trees! The warmth and fragrances of spring! A few birds fluttering and swooping above. Fellow humans leisurely strolling about, appreciating our shared good fortune.
You let yourself get lost in the delight of it. Off guard...*Ahhh*...
SPLUURG!
What, the?...
Oozing through your hair, dripping down your forehead. *Eeyuuck!*
What were the odds? I mean, *this shouldn't be happening*. I mean, the ONE loaded bird—way, way up there—and out of *thousands* of square feet below—it's as if the bird actually *aimed* at the single square foot you occupied. Can a bird *do* that?
The embarrassment of it. The—*shame?* To have been singled out—by the bird? By *FATE?* (Which is *sooo* worse! To deserve it.) Glancing surreptitiously around. Who else is aware of your ignominious dubbing?
So totally YUCKED—but can't act yucked, no no, that will surely draw attention. Just cooly and calmly, yes, yes, a casual wipe-off with your pocket tissue. *Nothing to see here!* The nearest water faucet? Why, oh, you *just happen* to be headed off in that direction...
Too late! You *had been* noticed! Must have somehow given yourself away. Could this get any worse???
Only one thing for it. Must decide—hey, this is funny. Turning the tables by laughing along with everyone else.
And laughing along *with fate?*
Which raises the question: If strokes of bad luck don't signify to be taken seriously—then

should strokes of good luck ever be taken seriously? As signs from Heaven—or God?—that the one singled out with good luck deserves their good fortune. Is more worthy than others.

As for you?—here, now. Well, all considered, the incident wasn't so bad. Trivial actually, and there's still much to enjoy.

Here's to your lovely, humbling, ever-so-funny day!

APRIL 20

To blow away a dandelion seed is to set a wish free.
To drift off!—aloft. Mesmerizingly.
Perhaps to twist, slicing in smoothly, catching *just the right angle* of light.
Another dimension of dazzle?
A wish transfixing
In fate.

APRIL 21

Misty blue and misty gold. A-blaze! the haze of color.
The fen, a haze of color.
Misty blue and misty gold. The far, expansive fen—a-glow
In a midday haze of
      Stagnation. Of browns, purples, greens—
      All a-blue, and in-betweens.
Holding wide.
A-far.

A-far the fen a-glow. A-far
      From morn.
        A-far from night.
        A-far from clarity.
An in-between of motion.—Death?
Wide in-between.
Life's misty breath.

APRIL 22

Chin up, Little Beaver! Nose out of the water!
That's quite an impressive branch you've got there.
Branch, heck, that's a *tree*, Little Beaver.
What are you doing with a *tree?*
Paddle, paddle, paddle.

Glistening little nose out of the water.
He sure *looks like* he knows what he's doing, where he's going.

Chin up! You can do it!
Paddle, paddle, paddle.

...So determined! So *SURE*.
We're so wanting to be sure along with him.
Allowing our life's doubts to roll away,
Out with the criss-crossed frenzy of ripples from the branches.
Our profusion of doubts—silkily and silently smoothing out further... further... away.

As Little Beaver, chin up, tree in tow, paddles off further... further...
Away.

APRIL 23

Lookie! Lookie! *Everybody!*

Dear *dear* Robin friends—

You've shared all of this with us, from the very beginning, from flying in with twigs and fluff as we prepared our nest in our first flush of excitement. You were there with us—helping us. Then the joy and accomplishment of each egg laid!

Then you let us be—simply, quietly *be*—for so long—*so so long*—and now—NOW—

THEY'RE HATCHING!

New lives—new baby robin lives!—coming into the world!

How did you know? Here you are! The sky a-flutter with your theatrical, empathetic excitement.

All of you, *our friends!* Our *dear* friends! Here for the best part.

For what is excitement but to be shared?

In a rousing mutuality of respect! Sharing an awareness that life is to be cherished! That with these new lives, each of our souls will be enhanced.

Awareness of life's thrill, life's value, yes!—

Heightened by realizing that the new little chicks might not have been. The egglets *might not* have hatched. Any number of mishaps could have befallen. Storms could have torn the nest apart. Predators—raccoons, or those brazen, thievious blue jays—could have decimated our precious eggs. All our worry and oh-so-careful tending might not have paid off...

And it still feels—unbelievable. *Too good to be true.* How could something as precious as life come from—*nothing?* Yet *in spite* of being unbelievable—

Lookie! Lookie! Here they ARE!

And the new little wonders themselves—each drying off and fluffing out and letting itself be known—
How much of the adult birds' overt enthusiasm and welcome is creating patterns in their rapidly configuring brains and psyches? As they start registering the fullness and complexity of the feelings surrounding them. This potential having been established back in the egg? And now filling out with life's details?
With life's songs!
Each little chick Robin—each one swelling with the life songs of others, and each creating their own personalized songs.—
To share! To swell, in turn, within all who listen.

APRIL 24

It can be said that all of nature is perfect, but if one component were to be singled out, let us consider the egg. The humble egg.
An egg is so innocuous. It just—lies there.
Elegant in simplicity of line, form, color. *Perfectly* elegant—but nonetheless, just lying there.
Not hurting anyone.
Yet...
Cannot each egg be regarded as a compository of the force and power of all of nature? Hardly innocuous! As in
Total *Wow!*—*POW!*—Nature revitalizing and replenishing itself!
ALL within each elegant, exquisite, deceptively simple—
Egg.

APRIL 25

The egg that didn't hatch is
      A bird that didn't find its mate.
      An insect that didn't twitch its antennae.
      A lizard that didn't sun itself.
So close.
A breath away from breathing.
A heartbeat away from thumping awesomely
Into this world—
ALIVE!

Alas, the almost-here lie defeated—lost—within
Their perfect little coffins.

APRIL 26

You exist. You ARE.

The odds were infinitesimally small, you know.

Your sire contributed *millions* of sperm to the single act of mating that produced you, and if he had altered his position slightly—or if your mother had—or if they had timed it seconds earlier or later—then the sperm that was to become you would likely not have connected with the available egg that was to become you. This could have happened so starkly *easily!* No you.

Lowering the odds significantly more, consider that this fortuity must also have happened when each of your parents' parents conceived them. If *either of your parents* hadn't been born —no them—no you.

...With *their* parents having needed to be here—ad infinitum, back through your extended family tree. Back through *all of evolution*.

All your *billions!* of ancestors, through multiplicities of small quirks of fate, each crossed paths with one another—and reproduced.

How infinitesimally small must odds get to become—a miracle?

So confounding! To pin down what constitutes miracles.

But if you are looking for a definition of miracle, try this:

Locate an available mirror. Close your eyes, carefully position yourself, open your eyes—

Voila!—in front of your very eyes—YOU! A miracle!

APRIL 27

The flower was here first. Surely.
The flower. A sleek, twisted curvature of orange, yellow, green—with shadows playing across
    the colorful curves as clouds pass overhead, as leaves and branches sway.
Bold, thin lines of white sepals, reaching *up*. Splashes of darting red!

The bird. A resplendent quetzal! Green, red, blue. Darting! Alighting within swaying leaves and
    branches. Sleek body, feathers—curving and twisting—
Catching snatches of shadow. Snatches of light.
White tail streamers. Red and blue petals—no, *feathers*. White, narrow—sepals?
Whorls of color and light! Was that a beak? Yes. No—feet. *No,* yes—ridge lines? A twisting of
    sleek pod...

Where does a flower leave off and a bird take shape?—
Or is it a bird leaving off and a flower beginning?
When, in nature's complex evolutionary path, does beauty draw breath and take flight?

APRIL 28

Time is hollow
When everything happens, but it doesn't,
Within the echo of an ever-expanding, silent chamber.
Reflections reflecting—nothing.
Formulas and frameworks—yes! Abounding.
The ever-simple, complex matrixes of—
Everything.

Everything in utter stillness. All the possibilities—a reality of possibilities.
Beauty within beauty alone.

APRIL 29

The hoot of the owl, in an emptiness of night, fills the emptiness with—sonorous-ness.
A deep sonorous-ness that echoes, within itself.
Smooth gray echoes.
Brown echoes—and speckled echoes—
In the space around branches, brambles—and the overhanging darkness.
In the chilled open space around each minuscule particle of air.

In the stillness.
In the forest.

Clear hooting
Catching, reverberating!—

In the warm souls of little animals.
In the cold voids of night.
In the forest.

APRIL 30

Pray, tell me of the dangers
That intercept our lives.
Of sharp teeth in the shadows,
And how our kind survives.

Of talons out of nowhere
That snatch us in our fear.
Plucking discordant melodies
That deep inside we hear.

We're plucked like notes in awful songs.
Please say we needn't sing along.

Our bodies raise up hackles.
Sensations just aren't right.
Pray, help me pay attention
To the nuances of fright.

MAY

MAY 1

Is there a rhythm in the wind,
A quickening of air,
That stirs the leaves to sing loud
In verdant vivant-faire?

What kind of songs would leaves sing?

They'd startle first, then rasper
What they have always known,
News of the Earth and of the Sky,
Of branches thick, moss-grown.

Go on...

Of new shoots green and tender.
A rush of soft hello. *Hellooo...*
Of mem'ries dark, and—LIGHTNING!
Hard hits of tremolo.

Don't know about this. Not hearin' anything...

With small songbirds alighting,
'Twould be in trees' roots and sap
To counterpoint bird melodies
With this, their pagan rap.

MAY 2

An array of blotches deep in shadow—blackness—cut holes in the fabric of the forest.
Exterior shades of darkness protest:
The blotches are *too* dark. *Too* black. *Too* void of leaf or twig—or substance.

Yet there they are—blatant and glossy—and every now and then let out a caw of protest of their
      own:
I am!
I am!
I am!

MAY 3

...*uuuh*-CHARK!
A walrus's sneeze is a place in the breeze
Where sparkles and brazenness lie.
      Where innocence floats,
          Suspended in moats
That pop with a deep-tinkled sigh.

MAY 4

When a long, low horizontal swelling of a wave breaks long upon its shoreline,
The world whispers, laterally.
In a lisp.
And in small crinkly smile lines that crease the face of a stern and ever-changing
Planet.

MAY 5

In waters deep and murky
(*Murky... woo—ooo—ooo—wooo...*)
Live blobby creatures dark and lurky.
(*Dark and lurky... Dark and lurky... Dark and lurky...*)
With bulging eyes and splurgy splotches,
Idling fins. And strange topnotches.
(*Murky... woo—ooo—ooo—wooo...*)
And swaying grasses woven through
With darting neon peek-a-boos.
(*Chime. Chime. Chime. Chime. Chime. Chime. Chime.*)
(*Dark and lurky... Dark and lurky... Dark and lurky...*)
Slippery slimies. Tiny chimies.
(*Murky... Murky... Murky...*)

MAY 6

Eerie, reverberating echoes in the ocean tell us where the ocean is.
And tell the ocean where itself is.
Its boundaries. Where everything within it—*is*.
The corals, the algae, the sideways scuttling crabs, the multitude of anemones and fishes and
        whales...
Their sounds. Plus sounds of the settling and shifting Earth beneath—
Surrounding and deflecting off them all,
In a flowing succession of patterns throughout the heavy, dense, dark water.
Pierced now and again by glinting, wavering designs of light from above.
That stop, abruptly, where the ocean defines itself.
Then resound back.
Within.

MAY 7

There are so many, many—countless?—ways creatures use their senses to survive. Senses that enable them to detect, then adapt themselves to the world around them (the *changing* world around them). Using whatever is there to utilize! Such as light—light that is sometimes *created by the creatures themselves*. Bioluminescence (when they do create it) can be found in select squid, jellyfish, beetles, glow-worms, and more.
Besides enabling sight, light is sometimes used as a heat source, to navigate, to detect or lure prey—or to keep oneself from becoming prey, such as when the lanternfish's glow confuses predators from below, blending itself in with the brightness above.
(Isn't this is amazing stuff?)
Plus, practicality aside, don't forget the sense of sight enables some creatures to aesthetically enjoy life. (Although it can be said that aesthetically enjoying life does serve a function...)
Then consider the nervous system—necessary to detect (and thus avoid) pain, and to know when injuries have occurred (so they can be tended to). It also registers subtleties of when it's too hot or too cold, and... our *very brains* are part of our nervous system! (Wouldn't be *us* without our brains!)
Senses—oh so necessary!
With there being *so much* in our world to detect! Think of all that hearing enables us to be aware of! And where does one's sense of smell fit in? One's taste receptors?...
Then imagine something that exists, that you cannot detect. An amoeba for example, knows not of sight—and as such amoebae are unaware of much in the world they inhabit. Because something cannot be detected, doesn't mean it doesn't exist!
Thus, to now consider—possible other-dimensional phenomena. We *do* live in more than our "known" three dimensions. Scientific formulations have identified that we live in (daily

functioning in) *at least* six dimensions. And by using the senses we do have and our intellect, there are clues of what those other dimensions might contain, and entail. Much guess work involved, and speculating,

But those with so-called extra sensory perception (E.S.P.) can hone and feel comfortable using telepathy, clairvoyance, precognition, telekinesis—with some *accuracy*.

There is also evidence that some non-human animals use E.S.P. freely—as part of their regular sensory apparatus. (Hence, it is not really an "extra" sense.) Check out telepathy skills of felines, select birds, octopi... and might some be utilizing clairvoyance? What else??

And one final thought: Do you suppose that things exist that our rich imaginations—*cannot* imagine?

MAY 8

Does your heart soar *up-up-up!* with dancing, inspired? But your feet, pulling *dowwwn,* all heavy
    and tired?
(*The hippopotamus splash! The hippopotamus splash!*)
Twirl until roundy,
Feet all a-poundy.—
(*Hippopotamus splash! Hippopotamus splash!*)
Plunging down under.
Burbling thunder.
(*The hippopotamus splash! The hippopotamus splash!*)
Stomp and have at it.
Roundy. Dramatic.
(*The hippopotamus splash! The hippopotamus splash!*)
Plunging down under.
Burbling thunder.
(*Hippopotamus splash! Hippopotamus splash!*)
Getting splashed is a blessing.
(*Splashing a blessing! Splashing a blessing!*)
Hipp-oh! Not resting. Hipp-oh! Not resting.
(*The hippopotamus splash! The hippopotamus splash!*)

MAY 9

Honoring mothers in general is different than honoring a mother in specific.
Any given *specific* mother might not deserve the honor. Take Sherilyn for example. Just because
    a body gives birth doesn't mean that body will willingly make sacrifices, be noble, be
    amenable to learning parenting skills. Not all mothers put their children first.
But watch the worst of them clamor to be honored on Mothers' Day! I've known one that went
    as far as expecting special privileges *before* having children, because "*some day* she
    would be the *perfect* mother."
Amazing that any of their peers acquiesce to such demands—especially those times when it
    involves overlooking those who quietly, dependably *are* good mothers.
It is the good mothers who deserve to be celebrated! And let's say motherhood in general—
    because there are countless reasons why motherhood has earned, and keeps on earning,
    such tributes.

Recognizing each mother as an individual, though, is key. Then *collectively* there are so many
    of them that it's obvious how essential mothers are to the continuation of everything that
    is commendable about humankind.—
Plus!—each mother needs to feel recognized and appreciated as the individual she is.
Which brings us into the territory of how, well... each mother has her quirks and idiosyncrasies,
    and well... shortcomings. Such being the nature of individuality. No mom is perfect.
Daughters especially can feel the sting of imperfect mothers—their relationships often being
    fraught—while the men in their family simply look aside?—wanting "the women" to
    take care of their problems themselves. (Which may well be a good idea!) But that
    doesn't mean the problems don't exist! Nor that mother-son problems don't exist.
The complexities of the issues can be sharp and baffling, but woven inextricably throughout

them is also the *wonder* of motherhood. Of something better—and *above*—the problems.
Here's to letting us all feel awash in the wonder! Doing what we can to sort through it—taking into account mother-child connections that may have begun in the womb!—but mostly so you can acknowledge and feel gratitude for everything your mom got right. She didn't have to! But if your mom loves you, she tried, and it can be gratifying—and sentimental—to picture the things she did get right.

Although (sadly) if you're in the minority whose mom didn't love you, perhaps there was someone in your formative years who filled in and nurtured you, who did love you.
To any and ALL these special women in our lives, let's raise a glass and toast them today—
C*heers!*—with hugs and thanks!
Mindful that all of us are in this together, and that—
There is something even better that can be done:

The best way to honor motherhood, historically and *forever*, is to treat their children fairly. *It is the conduct every loving mother has ever desired most!* For her children to be respected —!—that their rights and freedoms not be abridged—!—that they have opportunities, a healthful environment, adequate medical care, some nice things in their lives.
And for it to be publicly acknowledged that their children's very existence in this world is a joy!
THAT is how the world can appreciate mothers in general.
To do right by mothers is to do right by what is most important to them: Their children.

MAY 10

Love me, love my babies, says…
The cat.
And that is that.
You will *of course* help my litter be taken care of, says…
Your companion dog. So trusting. It is understood between you that *nothing* is more important.
The gentle loving cow licks her newborn calf. It is unsteady, trembling, inquiring. Is it possible
      for a mother's heart to be bursting more with pride? With a deeper sense of rightness?

MAY 11

Let's say your highest priority in life is to do right by your children. Or no... to do right by your spouse? Or by your church?...
Or to do right by *yourself*?
Everyone has priorities.
But let's say... what *if*... doing right by yourself means you must place a higher priority on your spouse? Or in order to do right by your church—they say to prioritize your family? Or to place your family or children first means you must first take care of yourself?...
Or if prioritizing your hobbies means your country or Team Earth must take precedence (in order to sustain the hobbies). Or perhaps top allegiance to Team Earth is necessary for your children's lives to be fulfilled...
What is entailed in *truly* knowing your heart? In keeping your life on track?

MAY 12

I give you the world,
Although you did not ask to be born,
Nor is the world mine to give. I know this. You know this.
I am not even your mother—I am your grandmother.
It can be said I gave you your father, and that he—and his she—gave you the world.
Except the world is not theirs to give, either. They know this. I know this. You know this.
It must be known.
Nonetheless—
Here is the world, in all its beauty and agony and glory, from me. To you.
And someday you may pass it on to your own children, and grandchildren.
And then you will understand.

MAY 13

How can anyone be complacent?
Isn't there always something, somewhere in the world, that isn't right?
What if the wrongness is right under one's very nose? Most are.
How can that person go on living as if they are a pleasant person—*la-de-da*—without acknowledging what is right in front of them? And then, go on to pressure others to overlook the wrongs also?
And why is their peace-of-mind *hailed?* What is to be admired about serenity when its bearer is complicit in injustices?—
Sometimes going so far as to feel anger toward—and *punish*—those who object to joining in with their blindness?
What happens when those objecting to participate are children? Is there a smooth, polite way for children to expose injustices? At some point they may (should?) become angry and *not admire* those who are harming others.
But while still a child, they are also being harmed.
As they grow, will they let go of their commendable sense of injustice, and of their anger? The pressure is on for them not to feel angry. They are being disliked for it.
Will they ever figure out what is going on?

MAY 14

A soul to soothe? From one to one.
Within each other's care.
Compassion rules! Sincerity pools,
Easing your friend's despair.
With strong resolve, an easy stance,
Small gestures, unabated.
Where comfort lies in deep warm eyes.
This truth! Perpetuated.

MAY 15

A puzzlement for you:
When is a religion not a religion?
An answer:
When it purports to follow the wishes of Buddha.
Because the ultimate goal of Buddha's teaching (do you know?) is for there to be no structured religion.
The complicated rules and practices in which his devotees engage are merely "suggested routes" to attain Buddha's goal—for each individual to have inner peace and harmony with the universe. There are a multitude of other possible ways this goal can be achieved, but over the centuries, agreed-upon routes have become locked in—
And are passed off by-and-large as a religion itself.
What would Buddha think?
Would he smile upon the formalized practices?
Would he be happy that people are enjoying the kinship of sharing the practices together?
Or—might he frown that his sampling of examples has evolved into an essentially die-hard religion?
His wish being to rid the world of the dogma of religions!

MAY 16

Solemnly holding something precious in your hands.
A sacred religious text.
In which single phrases or sections may undeniably be true. But the whole of it?
Or the whole of it may be true—the gist—but select excerpts in isolation might not be.
What is one to believe??
How to discern?

MAY 17

All the snug and cozy places we call home!
    Hidey-holes complete with fluff,
    Secret exits, choice foodstuffs.
    Where one feels safe.
Secure.

All the grand and sumptuous places we call home!
    Awesome halls and craftsmanship,
    Pride of place, fully equipped
    With snazzy chic amenities
Procured.

All the quirky places we call home.
    Who would have thought? No one but you!
    A place where colors rendezvous
    In niches, nobs, zany
Contours.

Yet all of this! however cozy,
Stylish, quaint, grand, chateausy.
Can't be a home—not bonafide—
Without warm salience inside.
Transforming a place into—*Home*.

MAY 18

I'll fly home to you.
And to my coop,
And my feed, and my friends,
And to the welcome you have made for me there.
You may tie a silly little tag on my leg
And take me far afield,
And I'll launch with all the thrill that's in my heart
For stretching out my wings
And for—*fly-yyy-ing!*
And for seeing far and wide!
And for expanding my heart wide...
Wider... *Widest enough...*
To experience the august freedom
Of flying to where my heart feels *the widest of all.*
Our home.

MAY 19

If you please, the manatees
Know who they are and what they're about.
Blending in with roots slimey, and stones strung out,
They navigate life's sludgy currents.
While claiming clear! their sweet demurance.

MAY 20

Behold! The *astounding magnificence!* Could there be anything more impressive... more immense... more strong... more grand... *than*—
The adult male elephant!
Hmm... Well... how about an *adolescent* male elephant?
(Okay. Will try again...)
Behold! The *adolescent* male elephant! Not only *magnificent*, immense, strong, grand—but also... intelligent!—and *supremely* so! *Supremely* intelligent! (...As per our adolescent male elephant.)
So intelligent as to be aware he is astoundingly magnificent, impressive, immense, strong and intelligent.
ACUTELY aware. As in, he's being hit with a super-nova jolt of testosterone (averaging about 60x base level)—lending credence to his brilliant new insight of supremacy. And borne mercilessly home with temporal pains equivalent to severe toothaches.
Our young bull elephant *is not* in a very good mood. This is the first time musth has hit him, and it translates into stormy defiance of all who don't see his new truth—
Which includes (*uh, oh*...) the matriarch elephants in his herd. The young fillies don't seem overly keen on his new self, either. Not too pleasing, that. What's going on? He's always been a reasonable elephant...
Although other male elephants (whom he would have sworn were also reasonable) aren't seeing his obvious new splendor either. Could it be time to rethink this?
Brazen defiance! NO! What's right is RIGHT!
But...
What if... Could it be possible—*no!*—but what if, just maybe—some of the *obviously inferior* old gents could help him out here? They've always been willing to help before...

Then—HORROR!—one of the kindly old males, who does happen to be more magnificent than himself (come to think of it...) delivers *another* unwelcome jolt. Even bigger than the musth jolt!—
Enough to whack him out of his ego trip.

Humbleness. Contrition.

But...
Not *really* defeated. No. *No!*—humbleness can also be defied—defeated! What's right, *is right!* There could still be a way to pull off his preeminence—a yet unknown supreme of supreme ways—that only *He* will be able to think of.
Trunk on high. HE'S the man!

MAY 21

To be carried along by might.
By a brute, mechanical force—of *might*.
A big heavy lover taking you along for the ride.

Chugging and surging.
Chugging and surging.
Chugging and surging.
Sometimes a whistle. *Hweeee!*

You find yourself alert to outlying vistas—of imagination.
Fields of cattle. (So much *implied*, but the fleeting wisps of thought trail off...)
Tractors and water tanks. (They mean *something*...)
Back yards. Swing sets. Laundry hanging out to dry.
So much of life—flashing by—
As if, now, you're *above it*. A voyeur. Flying past and above and observing life—but also as if
        you *possess* it all. Life—all of life!—is yours
Within the might. The heavy, surging might.
You are within it, while it keeps surging forth within you.
It *IS* you.

Chugging, surging—imagining.
Chugging, surging—imagining.
Chugging, surging—imagining.
Hweeee!

MAY 22

You've done nothing to deserve this particular comfort.
At least nothing you're up to comprehending.
It just—is.
The peace you're feeling. Just—is.
The beauty of life. It just—is.
You're being rocked, lulled.
...So peaceful.
The rocking, lulling
...Sublime.
Leaning in with
How it—is.

MAY 23

Luck looks in when you look away.
Don't ever try to catch her!
      Her ways are light and pleasing,
      Vaporous and teasing.—
Surrounding you. Uplifting.
But oh, don't look!—There is no luck.
It's you. Your input. Your spunk.
The Lady Luck, she knows she's there.
But when you do—
You're sunk.

MAY 24

Those who are disenchanted
Lack social wherewithal. Is there a way they could compensate for lacking social wherewithal?
It is different than being unlucky. The unlucky can develop a sense of humor about it and refrain from feeling they deserve so many misfortunes. Coupled with a gritty determination to persevere, they have been known to smile and get on well. (Aware that *maybe next time* their luck will turn…)
The disenchanted bear personal responsibility for getting in over their heads. For not having thought things through—or in time—or clearly enough. It's not that fate's odds are stacked against them so much as they have stacked themselves against themselves—
Which keeps playing out, over and over, as time goes on.
If that has become your life pattern—consider changing it! Rearrange the stacking. When your niche in life, apparently, isn't working for you. Such as by maybe changing jobs to one that's a better match for your abilities, where you can be more competent. So you can feel more useful.—
Or switch out your friends. Or where you live. Somehow—with an eye on prudence—establishing some new patterns of interaction that better suit your personality and who you truly are.
Then, once your true self is more in the open, you'd be bringing more honesty into the equation. Will be better able to sort through your thoughts. Better able to recognize life's—enchantment.

Not that rearranging your life situation will give you social wherewithal. Some people are just incapable of it. (Sorry.) But you don't have to play into being disenchanted!

MAY 25

If you feel like you're a nobody, how to start feeling like a somebody? (Not that you do feel like a nobody, but *if ever*... just in case...)
1) Realize it's up to you. Not to depend on anyone else—or *anything* else—to create the feeling for you.
2) Develop integrity.

MAY 26

The hop of the bunny
Is every good thing springing up into life.—
Each edible flower, each sweet blade of grass. Each friend.
Its hop is the path away from predators—
And taking the *leap up!* into sunshine.
The hop of the bunny
Is each person being the best they can be,
With tail, a-fluff and thick.
And as you reach *your ZENITH!*—
You're its fierce and feisty kick.

MAY 27

Welcome to our performance of "Meadow Medley." A new day is dawning, and we ask you to be quiet, please, so you can hear...

RIOTS OF FLOWERS
WITH COLORFUL POWERS.
WE! are the flowers.
We sing! [*with bells and harmonics*]

SLY, HEALTHY FOXES
OF PARADOXES.
WE! are the foxes.
We sing! [*with soft thumping—snarls?*]

QUICK KANGAROO RATS
ARE JUMPING ACROBATS.
WE! are kangaroo rats.
We sing! [*in quick words*]
We *JUMP!* [*quick music*]

I am a boulder.
A silent beholder.

GRUMPY FAT TOADS
LOVE MUDDY ABODES.

WE! are the toads. [*rasping guiros*]

[*repeated successions of dancing and songs*]

I am the boulder.
I keep getting older.

[*briefly more merriment, then all together—sans rock*]
The meadow is alive.
WE SING!

FURRY SOFT RABBITS
OF GENGLE SOFT HABITS.
WE! are the rabbits.
We nibble grasses. [*with clicks and soft chimes*]

[*the rock*] Time passes.

[*the rabbits*] We nibble grasses.

[*fading into silence—then slowly, dancing revives*]
[*quietly everyone resumes singing their part—sans rock—ascending, ascending, until...*]

THE MEADOW IS ALIVE!

~ ~ ~ ~ ~ ~ ~ ~

About the songs: Each group has made up their own. For example, the flowers might tell about the sun or elaborate about their color powers, or about their roots. Sung to the music, but rhyming not necessary. Or just la-la-la's, if that's what they have to say.

The foxes might tell of their cunning, or how they spend most of their day—perhaps pantomiming it.

Some of the songs might incorporate refrains of "The meadow is alive."

Toads get to croak randomly.

Be careful when adding extra embellishments (if at all). For example, a motionless silent "sun" might stand throughout (if you have an exceptionally shy child), or a younger sibling could flutter by—once!—as a butterfly.

MAY 28

Getting ready for Memorial Day? It will be here soon! (If not already...)
Got your barbecue set up, patio hosed off, groceries purchased?
This holiday marks the unofficial beginning of summer!
It is also a time to keep in mind what is *officially* being celebrated. The honoring and mourning of U.S.A. military personnel who died while serving our country.
Often confused with Veterans Day, which honors ALL our military personnel who served—not only those who died while doing so, and who may in fact still be living.
Both holidays sometimes being confused with Labor Day, which celebrates those in the U.S.A. who labor—including military personnel, as that is one of the types of labor.
I am taking a deep breath here—and advise you to do likewise. It can be satisfying to know what is being celebrated, and today's composition will address *all three* holidays—and not just regarding those here in the United States of America, but for *anyone* who died for their country—*throughout history*—and for everyone who labors, emphasizing those who perished while doing so. They all being worthy of recognition!

To start—with those who labor. To acknowledge and thank them, one and all. *But*—what if their labor was forced?—not of their own free will. Is it appropriate to thank someone under those circumstances?
Picture in your mind assorted "wonders of the world"—the great Egyptian pyramids, the Taj Mahal, our U.S. White House and Capitol monuments...
Picture the great Transcontinental Railway, linking the far shores of our country, the engineering feat of the Roman aqueducts, the Great Wall of China. A list that goes on, and on.
Then picture the workers upon whose backs these marvels were constructed. Imagine their injuries, their suffering—their deaths. Bring to mind their families, also suffering to accomplish... what?

Were the laborers and their families in-the-spirit of the project, willingly taking their chances to contribute to an achievement they would be proud of?
If so, then surely let's thank them! (Given that the result is something we, too, value.)
Or if not for emotional satisfaction, do you suppose they might have been compensated adequately in other ways?—such as by having food, shelter, or experience provided. And they willingly agreed to the deal.
A thanks for that also?
But what, let's ask, constitutes "willingly agreed"? Supposing their acquiescing came under duress, because the alternatives available to them were even worse.
Or what if their communal accomplishment, in the end, proved worthless?—(so many historical examples of this!)—or worse, what if their final achievement was something detrimental or repulsive to what they valued? Such as monuments to a religion they consider immoral, or helping produce war implements to bombard their own people.
How could someone possibly welcome thanks for having contributed to something like that?

What—if anything—*do* we owe to the memory of the countless numbers of nameless, faceless forced laborers who have passed through the chain of human history?
An acknowledgement, perhaps, of how life had been unfair for them?

And what of the countless casualties of warfare throughout history? To those who sacrificed their health and lives willingly, for a noble cause—then, yes!—a hearty thank you! But how many more suffered and died unwillingly—conscripted or otherwise trapped with no better alternative than to participate?
And what if what they considered "noble" at the time they might not think so if they could come back and be alive today, with a new and better understanding of the situation?

Here is one suggestion for how to memorialize laborers and those who made military sacrifices: In songs. *Music!*
Songs we compose and sing in their honor—and also songs to keep alive, keep singing, that they sung while performing their tasks and enduring their ordeals. To the best of our ability, to reconstruct those songs. Singing them in empathy with the reality of their experience, but mostly—oh, so mostly!—to celebrate the glory of what the human spirit endures, right along with them, and through them. And...
In thanks to them. For their part in human glory.

MAY 29

Dazzling!

A dainty blitz of avian iridescence,
Splintering sunlight
Into a thousand piercing charms,
Flung out spinning into the world around—
Around—
Into a sanctity of xylophonic
Glow.

MAY 30

The odds of meeting you were slim—
Impossible, they'd say.
      Yet there you stand; I by your side.
      So real in cohort, groom and bride.
      Saying our vows this day.
Wonder kept odds at bay.

The road ahead will test us both,
The realists do remind us.
      Yet skills are real; we'll learn, be led.
      Always there will be hope ahead!
      Problems, they can't untwine us.
The wonder is what binds us.

We will hold tight, we vow, forsooth—
Forever, and a day.
For in that extra day there lies
The wonder of our truth.

MAY 31

Inhaling the scent of roses during infancy in the quiet sun-sauna of the family garden...
Is to smell roses under the trellised gazebo of your hometown library, while lost in a book of faraway lands and emotions...
Is to inhale the delicate, perfumed scent of rose on your wedding day, as new securities and exhilarations open up before you...
Is to meld each memory together with the singular, subtle, essence of rose.

JUNE

JUNE 1

Butterflies!
Fluttering! Vibrant kaleidoscopic
Glimpses of color.
Floating in wispy loops—
To a destination? Just randomly ending up—where they want to be?
Ditzy flips of sateen wings and itsy shadows.
Up!—Quick-down!—Color flash!
Not quite beguiling, but close enough—
Not quite enchanting, but close enough—
To tease us that they are.

JUNE 2

Hey, I can slither on by if I want to.
Excepting I didn't.
What you thought you saw wasn't me.
I'm faster than that.
Excepting I wasn't.
'Cuz I didn't.
And that last departing slip of a tail?
A quick suck into a vacuum
That isn't—
That wasn't—
Not me.

JUNE 3

Wiggly, squiggly polliwogs,
As living modern art.
A multi-layered abstract
Of headstrong glints and darts.
Framed in a mat of reeds and mud
Banked up in washed-out logs.
We'll leave our little brush strokes
As they burgeon into—frogs!
Riiibbit.
And now the picture hops away—
Adieu to our trouvailles.
To come: The story's secret end—
What happens to their tails.

A fairy (*Hail! a Fairy!*)
Collects these tiny strips.
She flits among the reeds and logs
For her kinky, chic—hairclips!

JUNE 4

Truth in art
Is truth of the heart.
As envisioned first by the artist, then seen by the beholder.
Or not seen.
Or for the beholder to experience their own truths, as jogged by the vision of the artist.
Or not jogged. But enjoyed in their own personalized way—
Which, when experienced by many, adds up into a collective whole,
With multiple other treasured components, culminating in—
Culture.

Culture, which is then experienced by new individuals who were not part of the original forming
  of the culture,
But who now enter into it also.
Is this where you fit in? As a beholder of the collective visions of others, then selecting down
  from there to particular works of art that most please you?
Whether you enjoy paintings, sculptures, theatrical performances, musical compositions,
  literature, photography, films, architecture, folk crafts…
Seeing in them, truth.
Experiencing through them—yourself.

Or is any interest you have in the arts not as an appreciator, but as a creator?
With the media of your choice at hand, to transform what can be viewed realistically into "how it
  is supposed to be seen." *Your* truth. Your drawing, your story, your music, your
  photograph…
Of infinite possibilities, to lock in—forever—one sure distinction
Of human cachet.

JUNE 5

Who all has said that children are simplistic and unappreciative of the nuances of art and culture?
    Certainly not anyone who has ever associated with and paid attention to children! The youngest of them. Babies. Toddlers.

The music these littlest of ones are most drawn to have structure, rhythms, melody, harmony.

The children rouse, cheerfully clapping and wiggling to nuanced, merry tunes. They settle to classical music of the highest quality.

The visual arts that most intrigue them have a perfection of color and form. The best of it! They catch the emotions.

And—*of higher importance*—they can distinguish sincerity of emotions in the people and animals around them. Clearly.

But then somewhere along the line—around their threes or early fours—to varying degrees they become self-conscious of it and zero-in on the more simplistic and crude. (It is also the age when their sense of humor takes an interesting turn!)

But not to think *they* are simplistic! As they age they are still aware, on an underlying level, of their earliest intuitions—and can tell when adults are talking down to them. Or when adults are throwing inferior stories, music, and art at them, as if they had no depth. (Not that they don't sometimes enjoy crudity, but you're supposed to be in on the fact that they're playing around with it. In control!)

Those children who are most reluctant to let go of their early insights and abilities (but who, of necessity, let go to some degree) are those we label "gifted."

The word "stubborn" may also come to mind if one is trying to manipulate them into seeing life, and art, another way.

Just remember—helping children keep in touch with themselves, especially their gut recognition of sincerity—Yes!

They're our fledgling aficionados of... *Life!*

JUNE 6

To hop. To go from point A to point B in a bold and fulsome fling.
To fly!—up and far in a clipped moment of forever. Time—stop.
Time—resume! *Pa-plunk*.
So much for flying. Now a moment of grounded reality. Until?—
Over there, that's my place!
Pa-fling! Plunk.
Pa-fling! Plunk.
Pa-fling! Plunk.

Consecutive fulsome moments of—claiming one's place.
One's place. Now here. Now there.
Why—it's in the air!

JUNE 7

It hops. It scurries. It flutters its wings.
It'ssss... dinner!
The thrill of the chase! The challenge. The adroit fine-tuning of hunting skills. The... THRILL OF SUCCESS!

Is it possible you could, maybe, JUST STOP gloating like that? Speaking of your dinner as mere objects.

It's my right to gloat, and to speak as I please. It's my right to eat! And to be clever and skillful. It's my right to be who I am and to enjoy life. TO BE A WINNER!

Try—it's your right to fail. To be a loser. To go hungry. You could even become weakened and preyed upon. YOU could be someone's dinner.

No no, oh no. Those aren't rights. Those are fates. Fates for others.

If they have fates, have you not a fate?

A good one!

Just—okay?—stop gloating. And in case you haven't noticed, those enticing little things have now hopped, scurried and flown away.

JUNE 8

When ominous darkness steals the day,
Keeping swelling buds at bay—
     Hear the heavens roil with thunder!
     Hear them, striking hopes asunder.
Yet...
Beauty finds a way.

When going forth leads one astray,
To wander, hurt, in disarray—
     Then doom creeps in like vultures pleading.
     Blocking sight of others leading.
While...
Beauty finds its way.

When one looks out through sordid fracas,
And sees where caring ones long to take us—
     Then shrouds of darkness draw aside,
     And thwarted blossoms open wide!
Let...
Beauty find a way.

JUNE 9

Just a wink away—from a conspiracy.
So quick—
Wink-Wink! To catch it,
And to be caught—in someone else's
Twinkle.
Wink-Twink!—
Now yours! Instantly expanding.
Within a glint,
Deep depths of understanding.

JUNE 10

To stand atop a cliff, alone, under the starlit sky.
You. Cliff.
Starlit sky.

In that moment, you're sobered with the knowledge that you survive in life
...Alone.

So alone it feels as if the quiescence that's filling the universe
Is also inside you,
And that your howl that fills the night air makes no difference.
It is of the same air.
The same quiescence.

JUNE 11

The will of a gnat is no small thing.
It wrests free of its cocoon! Stretches. Takes wing!
It locates what's tasty with focused propelling.
It mates!...
With *GINORMOUS* compelling.

JUNE 12

Ornery.
Over two tons of muscle and might,
With a battering horn on front.
Are peaceful moments enjoyed?
Is might right?
Is there such a thing as animal porn?
It seems a big gray rock will do.
Are we really dared to not look away?
Does making a fool of oneself not register?
Any claim to finesse is left behind
In slimey puddles on the rock.

JUNE 13

An earthworm's solace:
I feel every wee vibration of earth around me.
They are my music.
They inspire me.
They sing confidently of everything there is to know.
One could not know more comfort.
I move and live and die within the song of Earth.

JUNE 14

X - X - X
Exuberant
Extreme
Exercise.
Pushed to your limits! Physical exercise:
      How many pushups can you do? How fast can you run? How well do you play sports?...
Mental exercise:
      How much knowledge can you amass—and what sense do you make of it? How well can you solve problems?...
Spiritual exercise:
      Sky's the limit!
Pushing yourself to the outermost limits of your capacity. Acknowledging that capacity!—yet by pushing it, you stretch it. Then drawing back at intervals into your comfort zone.
When riding the edge—the razor edge of your abilities, abutted with danger—it can be
Exhilarating!
Exhausting.
You become aware of your own unique style and what's really inside you. Your genuine
Extraordinary—
Exciting—
Exceptional! self.

JUNE 15

They've grown up!
They're graduating.
They do.
The children who we may have thought were ours, never were, really, and if we put off facing that before, now comes the bitter-sweet moment.
We can be proud of them (certainly!), but you can also be proud of yourself for whatever help you provided along the way. But back to them—(this is about them)—
It is because they allowed you to help them, that you were able to. And whatever success they may have made of their life up to this point, and however much you may have helped, hindered, or possibly severely messed them up—from now on it is up to them. To take their situation in hand, whatever it is.
Time for us parents to draw back and consider ourselves—out of it.
A child may choose to keep you in their life, or perhaps cut you off while they establish an inner equilibrium. Until they feel confident they can deal with you, and be accepted, as an equal.
That's something else to be proud of them for! If they're not letting themselves be pushed around.

And then comes... the *BEST* part! It's when life starts going well for them—*if* that happens—it's such a sweetness. If so, sometimes then, in a mood of generosity, they might even want to give you credit for it—for *their* achievement! How generous is *that*?
But *YOU* will know it's not true. You must know that whatever they will be getting right in life, the bottom line is that it's their doing.—
And once they're *sure* you know this, it's the reason they might feel secure enough to pass over some credit to you.
It is also the reason it's not your fault when, as an adult, your child might screw up. You are no

longer accountable for their gains—or for their failures. (Some relief there, but sadness mostly, when their lives don't play out well.)

You can be *oh-so proud* of your child, though, for presently becoming a new adult! Proud of them for every good thing they've ever done, and for every potential good thing they are capable of doing.
Hats off to them! Today, their Graduation Day.

JUNE 16

Get ready! I'm a-comin'!
Holdin' steady—then *varoom!*
It will be so pleasant for you—so perfect—so fun.
Have been hiding glowing plans up my sleeve—*heh-heh-heh.*
We're on the eve!
You'll come along? This shan't go wrong!

(It can't—can it? Go wrong? *NO*—stop!—can't think like that. Can't doubt myself *NOW*. Not now, after *all I've gone through* growing up.)

This *shan't* go wrong!
All bets are on!
(They're on—what?—ME! *Yes!*)
All bets are on!
Get ready, World—
I'm HERE!

JUNE 17

There is perhaps nothing more elusive—or more disconcerting—than success.
You desire it, set it in your sights, hope for it—but *what is it?*
Take care in defining it. That's the only way you can know when you achieve it.
Be prepared to change your mind on what it is, perhaps many times over, whenever it doesn't
      feel—right.

Do you know the difference between being a success in life, as a human being, and being
      successful in career trajectories?
A journey awaits you—which could abruptly end at any moment. Would you consider your life
      a success if you died tomorrow?

JUNE 18

What is this? An answer? No. A possibility—wild and free!
Waiting for your question.

JUNE 19

In moments of dejection, you might ask yourself, "What's the point in creating something to last forever, in a world where nothing lasts forever?" Which would be assuming that your creation will not last forever.

Consider the archeological ruins of ancient civilizations. There once existed well-loved homes, gardens, cuisines, musical instruments, frescos, textiles… all the accoutrements of lives lived. When made, were they intended to last forever?

Some objects outlive one's lifespan, and some may survive many generations. Monuments can be long-lived, with artwork and stories etched in stone, which enshrine values, histories and ideas.

Our current values, histories and ideas tend to be enshrined in books, movies, museums, thumb drives, "in the cloud."

When we stash away for keepsies what we honor and cherish, how long do we envision it lasting?

Earthquakes jolt and shatter, pandemics kill, floods wash away, radiation and fires consume. In approximately five billion years, it is speculated that our trustworthy sun will bloat out, then compress, precipitating the end of our solar system. All other solar systems throughout the universe will also meet their annihilation.

Is there *anything* that lasts forever??

How about—if you establish love and loyalties—might they last forever?

Ideas maybe? Thoughts? Thoughts that went into, and are manifested within, personal decisions, experiences, *creations?*

"Forever" can be a baffling concept! Every moment of time—once it exists by something happening in it—could that be undone? Let's say it can't. And if not—then whatever happened in that moment would become part of "eternity." Every experience, accomplishment, emotion, every idea inherent in every creation made by a living being could well be etched—forevermore—in dimensions other than those currently known to us, in a manner unknown to us.

These thoughts being speculations. The intrigue of the possibility of such speculations!

As such—whatever discouragement you might presently be feeling, and if you're thinking in terms of eternity, perhaps the question to ask yourself is not, "What's the point in creating something to last forever?" but rather, "What's the point in *not* creating it?"

JUNE 20

The web of a foot is a glide through the lake,
With discarded footsteps rippling in its wake.
With clear orangey skin and a daydream to match.
Snippets of music. Firm churning thwacks.
The web of a foot is a quaint burst of freedom.
The finishing flair of a quack.

JUNE 21

HhhRishshshSHSHT!
A dragon! For you—your very own dragon.
Every life should have dragon in it once in awhile.
So—how about today?
HhhRishshsh! (Down, boy!)
Hear its assertive, deafening roar.
Claim this roar!
Flames! *Hhhhhst!* Fire!—
Yours!
Ferocity!
Fan wide your wings! Snake up your head! Slap your tail!
You got this!

JUNE 22

I am rarely (personally) a dragon (if it was between a dragon and a duck, hope you're seeing more of a duck), but I've been in your life for, oh gosh, coming on half a year now, and these daily verses have gotten more personal (and more demanding of you) than originally intended. And I, *umm*, mean to keep it up, so to be fair, and in the spirit of full disclosure, thought you might like to hear some of my, *ummm*—(okay)—faults.

(Ahem.) (Yes.) (Where to start?) If you were ever in a business meeting with me, you'd probably not like it too well (especially a middle-management meeting). I'm aware most folks like their voice to be heard, but oh gosh, so much wasted time. (At least *I've* got better things to do.) I tend to cut people off, as in—please just get to the point!—so we can—*leave!*

Then (you may have noticed) I can come off sounding like an authority on far more subjects than one person could possibly be an authority on. I do have *opinions* on many subjects—and relay observations—but not good on details—

And am *certainly* not an authority in any branch of science! Quite the opposite—although can you tell I love science? (*Totally* love it!) Am just unable to walk around with all that fascinating knowledge in me, as part of me. I can memorize basic information long enough to

pass a test, but then after the test, out it goes.

Regarding those who do walk around knowing so much (maybe you can guess this) I am excessively attracted to a few select ones—male scientists—especially naturalists and physicists. All wobbly knees here! It's just that *I* am not a scientist.

Nor am I hale and hardy. (Do I mistakenly give that impression too?) I'm game for a lot of physical activities and sports, and try them to see what they're like—but good at them? Not since my youngest years. Am now prone to fainting, sensitive to temperature fluctuations, light, pain, and see no point in (avoid) adrenaline rushes. Calm, everyday life provides enough adrenaline hits for me.

Hardly a paragon person here. I *especially* don't have the answers to all life's questions!
> Although I fancy I am good at *asking* questions. (I know—I know—any preschooler can ask questions…) But consider that when life's questions are phrased accurately (my forte!) then life's answers have a place to fall into. A motto: Let's get the questions right!

I am quiet—a listener and observer rather than a talker—and do sincerely like people. Think I'm getting that right.

As for things I feel shame about (really am hiding my face here—but here goes…). I'd love to be vegetarian, and admire those who are, but am prone to slipping up.

And I fluster easily, mixing up names and faces; can't keep a tune; am all-left-feet when it comes to dancing; and get lost, so helplessly lost, within anything technical.

May your strengths be sustaining, your qualities shine,
Your shortcomings short, unimportant, benign.

JUNE 23

Regarding those (drat) business meetings. An aspect worth addressing about them is when manipulations take place.

The most blatant example I have encountered is when a meeting was called after-hours (as in, no pay) to decide an issue *that the facilitator had already decided.* She had already placed.the orders when she made a big to-do about how she *needs* to hear "*each* of our opinions, how they are *each vital* so she can make the right choice." Then, one by one, we were forced to say something—for however long it took to say it.

If you were required to attend such a meeting (or made to feel you weren't a good sport otherwise, although "oh no, you don't *have to* attend"), do you know what your feelings would be?

Would you resent it, feeling disrespected? For having been asked to participate under false pretenses. For having been LIED TO.

Would you, for the sake of company harmony—and perhaps for keeping your job—go along with it?

Might you even decide—why not enjoy it? Just relax, enjoy the social or career aspect, maybe some donuts, and hey—having the stage for a while, with everyone attuned to you—not so bad. After all, every job has a downside—if the mandatory attendance *even is* a downside.

Here's the danger in deciding to go along with it: By accepting for yourself that manipulation is par-for-the-course, it puts you at risk for not caring when you manipulate and take advantage of others.

JUNE 24

To a longtime dear friend:
You've written another song? This means there is one more person you love, because they are
    who you compose songs about.
And it will be another good one, because *ALL* your songs are good ones, because every person
    you love is special. Not sure how you do it—know who to pick. It is
A gift.
And a gift you share. Via your songs about them.
Hopefully you know to not listen to those who don't realize this, and who might compare your
    compositions to all-time-greatest hits. Such critics might judge your singing
    unimaginative, simplistic, childish.
They mightn't know every adjective is precise, cutting straight to the soul of what's special about
    your newly embraced one. In just a few stanzas! That are lovely.
Because you are lovely.
You sparkle!

JUNE 25

Hey, Clever Spider, weave me a web,
Of silky intrigue. With neat, glist'ning thread.
Teach me your secrets.—I'll never tell!—
How we colluded. Why some were felled.
Snag me a morsel, twitching for freedom.
Is this where we pounce?
Is this where we eat him?
Hey, Clever Spider—HEY!—it's *ME* you've caught!
Your intrigue well-woven.
Your secret, uncloaken.
 (*Twitch. Twitch.* How did this go so wrong??)

JUNE 26

Hey, Winsome Gazelle, show me how to leap.
How to *swee-eeeep*
The sky with agility and grace.
I would be ever-so obliged,
And humbly surprised, if you will.
(*Oh, thank you!*)
The secret is in the running momentum? In the—
SPRING! Up we go!
Above life's obstacles and frivialities.
A-WING! With all that is open—
And fundamental.
And sheer.

JUNE 27

Hey, Awesome Elephant, will you teach me of majesty?
Or is it not wise to ask you?
Oh, I see, it is *not wise*. But that I doubted the wisdom of asking—that was wise?
Umm... Umm.. *Wisdom?* Could wisdom be a component of majesty, then?
I'm on the right track here—I feel it!—but why are you looking at me ever-so patiently?
Patience, then?—No, no, not patience, but learning *when* to be patient, and *when not* to be patient. Yes! Got it. (*Thank you.*)
Umm... One hears this a lot... That being responsible for oneself is a component of wisdom-?
...No! Now you are addled with sorrow. Shall I go away? I'm ever so sorry to have bothered you.
You're *laughing!* You're laughing because I started feeling sad also? (*I didn't know elephants could laugh—*
But this is a different kind of laugh. It's a sober laugh of understanding. And of joy.)

Yes, yes, now here we are both sober-laughing and shaking our heads. This is indeed too much.
Good-bye, then. We're off!
It was majestic to have met you, also.

JUNE 28

I admit to a compelling desire to stick my tongue out at you and hop-and-dance about, making further faces at you. (Well, not *you*, dear reader, but the person I am addressing.)//
And declare victory. HA!//
Victory over you (the person I am addressing) who feels superior to me. To rub it in that you weren't able to quash me. Ha!//
But if I were to behave so immaturely, wouldn't it compromise my victory? There you'd stand, all prim and sneering down on my antics as *proof* that you're better than me. Any credible claim I'd have of being right would dance... dance... dance... away.//
In your eyes, you'd win.//
In my eyes—it's not fair! To have worked so long and hard, overcoming the obstacles that you, in your position of power, kept throwing up in my path, and *now*—against the odds!—*to not be able to rejoice?*//
In your face. (Ha!)//
Or could it be that this is an opportunity for me to claim further victory? By deciding you're not worth it. Not worth me compromising *myself*.//
Yet whatever I decide, either way—(*sigh*)—I'm stuck accepting you.//
Just wish you were a different person to be accepting. Someone who isn't so locked into their behavior—and into your false apologies.//
You did, yes, apologize, but it wasn't sincere. I know you don't like me, and that you'd do it again.

JUNE 29

How to make sense of something that moves so fast it's blurry?
To slow down a speeding object—such as a sports car—to look at it long enough to satisfactorily identify it.
Was it a Ferrari? A Lamborghini? One could make a reasonable guess, but what year was it? What condition is it in? Who was driving it?
If a moment of motion would stand still—*click!*—then your brain, not still, could catch up.
And what if bigger or more abstract things could stand still? The times when the world or your life situations seem to be zooming by too fast—*click!*—to give your brain a chance to catch up.
How to understand *so relentlessly much* that is coming at you?—
Or so little coming at you. The times when everything seems to be going *so slow*, so booor-ing, that one wants to burst out thinking ahead of the action.
Speeding ups. Slowing downs. The aligning of your thoughts with it all!
Then consider the times when the blur itself is a joy. A streaking comet! The fun being the...

Stop! Cut! Was that a roadrunner that just whizzed by?
Drat! Missed it! Sure would love to see a roadrunner.
When not paying attention, one can miss even the blur.

JUNE 30

Mole feet.
That's all they ever let you see.
Of course moles must have bodies, and rather ugly ones we're told, although if living underground, what difference does it make?
But those super-duper feet—they sure know how to dig!
Urrrr-ip, urrrr-ip, urrrr-ip.
Zigging and zagging smartly under the surface, leaving an elongated path of loose, aerated soil in their wake.
Urrrr-ip. One's coming this way!
Urrrr-ip, urrrr-ip.
Whoops, there's a plant in the way.
Whoops, whoops, whoops, whoops, whoops. Down it goes in jerky increments.
Urrrr-ip, urrrr-ip, urrrr-ip. Almost here!
Urrrr-ip. We must see him this time!
Little *ppfts* of dirt shooting madly into the air.
A tantalizing dusty cloud.
Look in close! Is he there??
The dust dissipates away *aaand...*
Whooped again. Duped again.
Just a single webbed foot, flinging up a few final flecks of dirt, signing off.

JULY

JULY 1

It's not just the tea and the luscious pastries.
Okay, we love the tea and the luscious pastries—
But we love more the context. The completeness of it.
The history. Feeling linked with all the ladies gone before who sipped and let down their guard and shared intimacies. And—
The ambiance! Wondering whose mind envisioned the architecture, those who constructed it, who it might have been who thought of the the charming interior touches. And such a pleasant location the owner was able to acquire! The landscapers who enhanced it—how lovely! this trellised patio we're presently relaxing in.
In a mode of savoring. Then—the tea itself. The sweets. The savories. The cooks back in the kitchen. The welcoming, attentive staff. (*Hello waiters, waitresses! Thank you!*)
All of this augmented with our own contributions to the ongoing legacy. Our own conversation, jokes, banter—including silent observations, such as spotting out those among us who are trying to corrupt the situation or otherwise harm others.
ALL OF US—past, present, future—who taste this thought-endowed fare—the *same* fare—and sip the comforting teas, the *same* teas.—
As if this snippet of life has value.
And perfecting the art of it.

...Which might include—if one were to aim for perfection, here—to allow for more of nature. So we could intermingle the experience with something grander. Maybe a gentle, teasing breeze? Songbirds? And *oh, oh*—see that low stone wall over there? If a roadrunner were to whiz along it, and we glanced over *at just the right moment*—wouldn't that add a splendid finishing relish?

JULY 2

On a dark and hollow night when moonlight pours down upon a rabbit, the world is hushed still
As the rabbit.
Nary a twitch. A wide-eyed stillness expectant of—anything.
The rabbit's silken silhouette is outlined with moon glitter. As if it's transfixed within an
    enchantment—and creating an enchantment.
—Alive with omens.
But good omens or bad omens? Glittering, glimmering affirmations of a divine world? If so—
    divine for whom? For coyotes, owls? If bad omens, bad for whom?
In this dark, hushed eeriness.
The bunny's glowing haunches are primed, on the ready. Expectations are primed.

We wait.

JULY 3

From indecision comes analysis and introspection.
From introspection comes self-doubt.
From self-doubt comes some of the best decisions that were ever made.

JULY 4

Imagine a place—a haven!—where you're free to live your life and raise your family as you chose, true to your judgment, your sensibilities, and your culture.
For the persecuted, the United States of America has long beckoned as such a haven.
But there is a price to be paid for living here. A deal. In return for one's freedom of culture one must accept the cultures and ways-of-being of all the other citizens.
Each adult gets to be whoever they want. To associate with and identify with whomever they want—
Provided they let everyone else do the same.
This nips and tucks multiple aspects of multiple identities and cultures—those aspects that persecute others. And by such nipping and tucking an entirely new umbrella culture is continually in creation.
The U.S.A. is sometimes called a melting pot of cultures, or that it's a consortium of set cultures striving to live together in harmony. Neither hits the nail on the head.
We are multi-racial, multi-religion, multi-gender, multi-*everything*. Our ideal—our goal—is "liberty and justice for ALL." Is that great—*or what?*
To value the United States of America is to value The Deal.

(Not to mention this basic give-and-take among others is something you learned in kindergarten —or *preschool*.)

JULY 5

It's something to see!
Compounds of nature's chemicals and processes being studied, comprehended—reconfigured
    —manufactured—and—
KAPOOM!
Spectacular fireworks in celebration of something that humans choose to celebrate.
KAPOOM! *KAPSSS!* Bam!-Bam! Whsssst... BOOO-M!

...Along with the correlating development of spectacular weapons to wield against that which
    humans wish to dominate or destroy.
BOOM! Bang! Bang! You're dead.
The spectacle of humans making spectacles of themselves.

JULY 6

What if humanity was teetering on the brink of a bright new era—and no one noticed?
Too many distractions of—wild and crazy technological innovations, artificial intelligences, complicated social media connections...
Too many problems—climate change, biodiversity issues, starvation, pandemics, inept political systems, wars...
When right under our noses a solution may have steadily been taking root.
Wherein problems are not untangled by higher echelons of power dictating downward, but by each individual having the resources to identify and address their own personal issues. Competent bottom-level-up problem *prevention*.
Countless generations of humans have fumbled through their personal lives doing the best they could with the advice, traditions, and resources they'd been given. But look around today! Breakthroughs in psychology and brain science have enhanced profoundly the available concepts and tools to help new generations.
A populace of emotionally healthy individuals, understanding themselves and feeling in control of themselves, could go far in taking the simmering, destructive edge off humankind.
Moreover, feeling in control of oneself enables that person to stand tall and proud. To feel—
Human.

JULY 7

Wait... wait... wait...
Were the preceding few verses talking *politics?* (frowny face) About a change in the world's socio-economic system? About—a discarding of traditions and customs??
Well, actually (*um... umm...*) for some... it is even worse. (grimacy face) For those with a vested interest in keeping their lives and culture the way it is, the preceding few days' observations have referred to a changing of rules mid-game.
This is not a fair thing to do to someone. For example, imagine bases loaded. You hit the ball out of the park! As you slide triumphantly across home plate the ump shouts "You're out!" New rules having just come into play.
Or you're stuck in traffic, inching along in a cordoned-off lane *like you're supposed to do*, when a lane opens up to the right and cars start streaming past, cutting you off.
Life is full of slights and affronts, mostly minor—but imagine if it's *your whole life* that's being disregarded. When all you were trying to do was play by the rules and be good person.— Working hard and earnestly to provide for your family, attending church services and heeding its spiritual leader, and endeavoring to pass on your values and favorite pastimes to your children.
Then further imagine—having made sacrifices to do this. Maybe you never much liked your job, or that it slugged a damaging wallop to your health. Maybe your frequently-patched-up basement won't stop flooding, or you don't get to dine out as often as other (less deserving) folk. Or your children are having a hard time. And you're stuck! Too late to change your job or make other major life changes. You've made commitments. You will live out your life standing by them.
Could this get worse for an honorable person?? Well... what if you start figuring out you were

loyal to the wrong people? And the possibility (to be rejected!—surely!?) that your entire adult life has been one big mistake. This *is not* how you want your progeny to remember you.

It is UNFAIR.

It would be. Unfair.

If any of these scenarios are happening to you as society keeps adapting to our changing world— as your way of life keeps getting nipped-and-tucked—please consider this consolation:

Any changes will probably come about gradually, in fits and starts, and assuming your top priority is your children, then the changes on offer should be to their benefit. So they won't have to make the same life sacrifices that you made. So they can have a better, more flexible, more fulfilling life. A *more fair* life.

And they would catch on, as children do, to your priorities (that you are putting them ahead of yourself) and how you are being a good sport. For *everyone's* benefit. You can shine—in the eyes of your children.

How's that for a lasting legacy?

JULY 8

On some days a high layer of compacted gray puffs cosset us here below,
Drawing one's eye upward to what can be a welcome, protective buffer between life-as-usual,
    down here, and "too much vastness" up beyond.
Allowing us each to focus undistracted on our immediate surroundings.
Although sometimes a small amount of vastness seeps through the day's soft, shadowy barrier to
    tug at our awareness of great secrets far and fleeting.
Of great challenges, unknown. Unmet.
Of what might induce insecurities, if we knew what dangers lie beyond our comprehension.
While down here, beneath a cloud cover similar to that of a warm blanket snugging us, we can
    feel free to look inward, into ourselves, tightly secure
That all knowledge, known and unknown, lies safe—*here!*—
Within each soul.

JULY 9

Facing west. Always the temptation to face west, where new adventures await. Stretching one's mind out past, past... the ever-further, further... plains and mountains and bodies of water to—
The Great Pacific Ocean.
It is there. You know it is there! Where waves swell high and crash against the rugged shoreline of loamy cliffs and massive, jagged rocks—carving out nooks and expanses of pebbled or sandy beaches.
And the water—such an immensity of water!—imagining within its cold depths a primal crudity wherein the elegance of Earthly life began.
The Great Pacific Ocean!
Where one's extending-out dreams end. Where one's dreams—come true?
Somewhere between the *here*, where we now stand, and the dramatic, alluring water far beyond —do dreams come true between the two? Or is it once you've gotten there, at your destination?
Along that long trajectory, if you were you to travel it physically, would the adventures and travails you experience be the fulfillment of dreams? Perhaps stopping somewhere along the way, satisfied, and making a life there.
Or is the dream to *be there*—to reach a goal! Having journeyed the distance, having paid the prices, to then pick your way down the cliffs, over the rocks, across the hot, disheveled sands—and *plunge!* headlong into the cold, salty sea.
Dream come true!
But if so—what next?
Or—could looking westward, *just the looking*, be enough? To follow the trajectory of your

thoughts along *their* journey? Suffusing yourself in the dreams along the way—perchance stopping midway, content. Or following your imaginings through, to—
The Great Pacific Ocean.
Dramatic. Eternal. Taunting?... Or satisfying? With its resounding, primal question: What next??

JULY 10

Illumination, warmth, brightness and... *Glory!*
Plants turning their leaves and faces upward to catch its nurturing rays,
Then bursting out into their own glory, and into sustenance for wildlife and humans.
Uplifted spirits! Bright new hope with each bright new sunrise.

Bright new clarity! Secrets revealed. As if everything is out in the open.
—*No secrets??* A dearth of illusions and subtlety?
Blatantness.

Fury.
Fury? *Fury!*—
Bold and brazen!
The fury of fire—tight, compressed fire—*raging fire!* Heat beyond our physical comprehension.
    —*ANNIHILATION!*
Relentless! Relentlessly blazing, the GIGANTUOUS sphere.
One must turn away from looking at it. From confronting it

With the triumph of our existence.

JULY 11

The multiverse: Unfathomed multi-dimensional space that contains
Our universe.
Within our universe—our solar system.
Within our solar system—our planet, Earth.
Within Earth—all our elements and their atoms.
Within each atom—unfathomed multi-dimensional space.
Space that is not empty. Just unfathomed. Space that contains—the multiverse?

JULY 12

The morning tree catches the first bright streaks of sunlight and—
Birds!
Preening birds. Convening birds.
Squawking and small-talking birds.
Fluffing, grooming. Bright! Festooning.
Shaking off droplets.
Toppling flip-flop-lets.
Animated within the illuminating streaks of light that are shifting smoothly through the branches.

JULY 13

The evening tree catches the sun's rosy afterglow and—
Memories.
Memories snagged in the myriad of bestilled leaves, among their shadows and recurrent flairs of color.
Memories of the day. Cherished memories of good times, past.
Memories quiet—hidden—among the leaves.
Then wistful flairs of color!
Memories softened. And scintillating.

JULY 14

Meep! Meep!
Roadrunners!
Sleek and slanty, zooming fast.
How long can sustained swiftness last?
Over rocks, through desert grass.
In jaunts of two—their mode.
  Turning, shooting past each other.
  Burning by each outcrop, gutter.
  Parting, quipping "bread and butter."
Relishing each road.

JULY 15

Meep! Meep!
Meep! Meep!

How many roadrunners does it take to sharpen a landscape into clarity?
When one's surroundings suddenly become "more real." More worthy of remembrance. A
     roadrunner was here—there—up—down—
Gone.
Zzzzzip...

Leaving
What else behind focused into sharper clarity?

JULY 16

This beautiful stray puppy. To be laid to rest.
And now to loosely weave a flower into its soft, wirey hair.
Was it loved by any—other than this human?
Perhaps—surely?—by its mother or a fellow pup.
Was its distinct personality and mind acknowledged by any other?
Would the pup appreciate the symbolism of the flower? Something beautiful, for the beautiful.
    Something singular—and precious.
When does beauty know, and not know itself?
In the gripping, gentle sorrow of doubt...
Be sure to put a flower in their hair.

JULY 17

Who's in charge here anyway?
Shouldn't the person who's right be in charge?
Perhaps it doesn't matter for select small projects, provided the projects get done well-enough, then, sure—let whoever enjoys leading do the leading.
But *overall* in charge? Of large operations—of countries and commonalities—of *life*?
Shouldn't someone who's right be in charge?
—Or at least right-enough to not cause damage!
But how to differentiate between qualified leaders and those who are woefully messing up? Who get it wrong.
Although... don't we all possess an inner core that can sense fairness, and truth?
And when that truth is violated, it is
Wrong. We feel it. Yet the wrongness may have become obscured under so many layers of superficiality that it can be tricky to pull to the surface. To be able to identify it.
Or one might settle into the superficiality, mistaking it for truth. Ignoring any nagging sense that it's not—then further mistaking their ignoring of it as being "tough." As commendable decisiveness.
Let's pull off any blinders, though, and see if we can identify what's going on.
Who's in charge here?

In your personal life, there may be those who have the gall to think they are *in charge of your heart*. As if your love is *theirs* to give to those *they* choose.
(So hard to believe it's happening that this can be hard to see. Read on...)
A dominate parent might try to claim credit for the attention and love the other parent provides—on the grounds they selected that parent. (A form of theft!)

A lover might not realize their partner's love is a gift they are giving, not an entitlement because they skillfully tricked that partner into falling in love. (A violation of not only one's heart and trust, but failure to acknowledge their free-will.)

Leaders of any group, large or small, might feel entitled to the adoration and blind faith of their constituents. Not appreciating the value of what it is.

Should we place our lives in the judgment of such thieves and bullies?

Back to the earlier proposition that power starts at the lowest level—in our personal lives—for each of us to see through such abuses and not give away our power to those who falsely claim they own it.

Doing so is what could lead us to having more qualified people "in charge."

JULY 18

What to block out of your life—and what to confront and deal with?
Some folks even block out that they're blocking things out. (Including maybe... blocking out this analysis?)
Some people do recognize when they are blocking things out, however (such as painful memories), but may not be aware they have a choice about whether to do so. It can help to know you have a choice.
The first step in knowing this is to acknowledge the existence of whatever it is you're not yet ready to thoughtfully weigh. (And may never be ready.) Just acknowledge that it's there. Maybe make a list of them. For example, a list might include the time a beloved person slighted you, or if you have a proclivity toward justifying why it's okay to hurt others. Things that might not be fun to look at—but hey, what exists, exists.
Next: Tick mark items on your list that you someday *might* want to confront and deal with,
Simultaneously noting those aspects of yourself and your life that you're happy leaving in the dark.
You will be making choices!
You will be adding to your self-knowledge.
Also, the choice of whether to consult a professional to help you in any stage of this. (There being so many excellent, qualified professionals available these days.)
Your life! Your choices! Your list.
(*My own list is rather lengthy, incidentally.*)

JULY 19

Meerkats, peerkats on the watch
For any sign of danger.
Standing high, forefeet held close,
Those they love held close—
Must protect them!
Know what predators do
And consciously aghast. *So wrong!*
So wrong! Look deep and long
Through astute eyes that pierce disguise,
And sort what's wrong,
From right.

JULY 20

An invitation (from whom?):

My eyes are round.
They are large.
Won't you look into them?
Let me take you in.
Come... As you enter, experience the world growing larger...
Larger...
As bewildering shapes and shadows come into focus.
Clearer...
As you become privy to my visions.
Expanding...
To the furthest evocations of vision's sphere. Vision's orb.

Within the orb of my eyes, an expanding orb of evocations.
Both orbs round and large.
Each within the other.
Won't you—enter?

JULY 21

Padded, fluid steps of discernment.
      Discerning the temperament of the object.
      Discerning the thoughts and weaknesses of the object.
Striking a pose.
Edging angles.
Shoulders low, hunched.
Taut, sinew-ous muscles at the ready.
Eyes wide—
Admitting the prey into its very soul.

Timeless, rapt composure.
Minute false starts.
Any doubt, any anxiety, released through twitches at the end of your tail.

JULY 22

A peacock's unfurled, radiant tail
Can dazzle from afar.
Spangled with an array of brilliant "eyes" to confound predators into believing they are being
    watched.
With exotic colors of a tropical explosion,
And iridescents that will be shimmered
Into glory.

But unless you are a she-cock,
Don't be fooled.

Glory is in the eye of the beholder.
As you stand transfixed, in awe of the spectacle—
Real eyes can creep up from behind.

JULY 23

Laid back.
Too laid back?
> *We don't know.*
> *We don't care.*
> *Whatever goes.*
> *Whatever's there.*

Are you overwhelmed?
> *Overwhelmed by what?*

Underwhelmed?
> *Not enough of what?*

WHAT
Is going on here?
> *We don't know.*
> *We don't care.*
> *Whatever goes.*
> *Whatever's there.*

JULY 24

I love that…
Rosebushes have thorns.
Spikey, thick thorns, those Rugosas, with the most delicate, sweetly-perfumed blooms.
Nature has outdone herself with Rugosa blooms!—But take care when reaching through the branches and bending in to inhale the scent.
Mother Nature doesn't welcome you picking them, either. *No-No!*—*a* reason for those spikey thorns—
On those Rugosas—
And on most wild roses. Leave nature to her defenses! In a world of hungry deer, assorted and sundry nibblers, diseases, freezing temperatures…
Defenses are to be admired.
They go hand-in-hand with—and empower!—life's delicate, ephemeral beauty.

JULY 25

Allow me to share with you:
The jocular father in the convenience store check-out line, with two bouncy (*super* bouncy!) children, one in the cart.
The man got a bum deal. The line to his left was moving a lot faster. Then a salesclerk opened a third line, further left, toward which new customers made a beeline—along with several crossovers from the line snaked behind him.
One of the kids noticed. "Hey Dad! They were behind us!" Followed by a younger, thinner voice whining, "What's taking so long?"
Mr. Dad, pleasantly stoic, "It is what it is." Then back to entertaining them with jokes and conversation about their shopping cart items.

What difference does a parent's attitude make? To themself, and their family? To the world?
Mr. Dad could probably contribute some prodigious thoughts here, but let's gauge the situation by the youngsters. Let's imagine them twenty years from now. Assuming their dad maintains his attentive, jovial, philosophic outlook—what effect will that have had upon them? How will it have affected the manner they come to terms with their own lives, and with their happiness?
They will be the ones to ask—in their adulthood—for their thoughts.
Until then, your thoughts:
What difference do you think a parent's engaging, pleasant attitude toward life has on their children?

JULY 26

Images of an empty sky reflect upward
From far expanses of sand, soil, water, and
From far, flat expanses of concrete, asphalt.
The sky reflecting invisibly back up
Into itself,
Enabling mirages within the invisibility.
Something—*etherial!*—
Pulsing and fluctuating in leisurely waves—these mirages—
So that at intervals we see more, then less, of whatever we're seeing.
That we shouldn't be seeing?
Because nothing is there!
So what *is* there? Only foolery? Illusions?
...Delight?

JULY 27

There's something unsettling about a camel.
Perhaps one should marvel at their efficiency in conserving water and how well their bodies have adapted to a harsh environment.
There is a curmudgeon complacency beneath their long eyelashes and square-set jowls chewing cud.
Way cool! So why... an uneasiness?
Perhaps it's their odor—musky (*cool!*) but often pungent and foul,
That doesn't settle right.
Perhaps it's the way they look at us. With disregard? With *contempt?*
Could their cud-chewing complacency be in rumination of not liking us?
Or perhaps it is something even more profound. That one of the harsh conditions camels have evolved to accommodate to, over more than five millennia, is subjugation and abuse by humans.
Unsettling, to be in the presence of what we have wrought.

JULY 28

To all the children of the world:
You are on your own to make the most of your life. (You suspected as much, so hang onto that insight!)
You are presently under the care of your parents or guardians, but are on your own to make the most of whatever that situation is.
Hopefully you *at least* have adequate water, food, medical care, clothing, and housing.
Hopefully you feel safe, loved, and are receiving *at minimum* a basic education.
Hopefully you are able to play, socialize, explore, and learn life lessons—with joy in your friendships and culture.
Your childhood will fall sort in some regards. Every childhood does. This is where making the most of it comes in!
The important thought to bear in mind is that, yes, you are vulnerable and others are responsible for your care, and yes, it is not fair when you suffer. *But never forget* your soul belongs to you, not to them.
You get to think whatever you want to think, and feel whatever it is you feel, regardless of the times you have to fake otherwise in order to keep receiving care. You are not a hypocrite when you do that as a child. (Only if you do it as an adult.)
Making the most of your situation during any conflicted times also sets you up to better recognize and appreciate the times your guardians do get it right. So you are less likely to take their efforts, skill, and gifts to you for granted.
Hopefully they get parenting right a lot!
If not, when you are an adult, please seek out support groups with those who have gone through similar experiences, or engage qualified professionals with skills that can help.
And while still growing up—remember it's never too early to look out beyond your immediate

family and their associates, and learn to spot out other adults who care, whom you may be able to turn to for additional support and guidance.

Legions of caring people are hoping you make it through!

JULY 29

Let it rain!
Drops bleat fervently onto our pup tent. *Oh, yes!* This is what matters! Anything beyond our tent
—doesn't matter.
The rapid-fire thunks obliterate anything beyond. Only we—together!—matter.
(*Let it rain! Let it rain!*)
You and me. Me and you. Only us. There is no other world.
We are strong! We are right! We are snug.
(*Within our tent... Within our tent...*)
(*Thunk-thunk-thunk-thunk-thunk-thunk-thunk...*)
So warm you are. So right we are. Everything right regarding everything clsc is within us.
(*We are what's right! We are what's right!*)
(*We are strong! We are strong!*)
(*Thunk-thunk-thunk-thunk-thunk-thunk-thunk-thunk-thunk...*)
Everything that is right will last forever.
(*Within our tent... Within our tent...*)
Let it rain!
Let it rain!
Let it rain!

JULY 30

A proposition: Reality for conscious beings is what we imagine it to be. *But* (the caveat!)...
We have to imagine something that is true.
Then it will become real. For us.
If no-one imagines it, it is a potential, but not real yet.
A lot of our reality is already established.
All conscious beings share a common reality. It is continually expanded (and possibly
　　　reinforced) as minds hit upon what is true.

A corollary would be: A definition of "right." When you create something unique and get it right,
　　　that is what makes it right.
A conclusion would be: Truth is the paradigm.
Definition clarification: Expansion can be not only outward, but also inward and
　　　multidimensionally.

JULY 31

The world of the river otter is the same world as everyone else—
With an extra dose of fun.
More slippery and slidey. See there!—
How it's done.
More umphy and triumphy.
More darey and flip-flairy.
More pertly on the run.
Overtly thinking-some.—
Then decidedly—(*quite so*)—
A chum!

AUGUST

AUGUST 1

The fortuity question:
Wouldn't it be fortuitous if what we enjoy most is also what's best for us? And vice-versa—
If what's best for us is also most fun?
Take exercising. Good for body and soul—right? Can you think of a way to make exercising optimally fun for yourself?
And eating healthfully. What if the foods you craved most were those that were best for your body?
Then there's employment—your job. Deeply satisfying?
Leisure time—*oo-ooo!*—here's something you might want to look into: Did you know there's evidence that some video games, when played appropriately, can provide as good a workout as having physically engaged in the activity that one is mentally engaging with? (Not that you'd want to *always* forego real physical exercise for them, but as a possible option for when it works best for you...)
Ask the fortuity question for *any* leisure-time activity. Consider the change of pace each activity provides. Refreshing? Varied stimulations that could, overall, lead to an up-tilt on life for you, first directly,
Then circuitously. Your stoked mood will affect those you interact with, likely boosting their mood also, which in turn could uplift those *they* interact with—perhaps getting back around to you. Lifting you even higher!
Could this be done in a manner so you're at peace with your conscience?
In what other ways might the ideals of fortuity be achieved?
Something to look into!

AUGUST 2

Looking westward from the Pacific shoreline, emerging waves swell high and roll in, breaking
    upon the rocky escarpments and sandy shores—where even frolicsome otters daren't ride
    the waves in. The breaking is *too wild*—
Too treacherous. *Too* much!
So rozen up your surfboard—this needs a beachboy touch!

The water—powerful! Immense!
The sun, a brilliant blessing.
Golden splendor shining through
Waves pulling back and cresting.

Respect the water's power! Absorb the glory of the sun!
Paddle your board into them—*becoming one!*
All merging with your skills, and aching—
Then—Oh God!—*THE OCEAN'S BREAKING!*

All as one!
All met. *Begun!*
Know peace.
Wild on the surf.

AUGUST 3

Jellyfish are New Age music
Manifested into a life form.
Surreal.
Languid, largo flitting.
Puffing out, sucking in.
Tentacles trailing behind, swaying.
Translucent translucency—
Of another world.
Puffing out...
Sucking in...
Tentacles trailing...
Otherworldly, yet a composed incarnation of Gaia—
Our Earth, our Gaia—
And her universal harmonics
Within.

AUGUST 4

A time-worn question: If a tree falls in the middle of a forest and no-one hears it, did it make a noise? (A better question would be—if a tree falls in the middle of the forest and no-one realizes it, did it really fall? We'll consider that next.)

The noise question. We're talking a *forest* here (right?), and forests are teeming with life! There's no way someone (*some* living being) didn't pick up on the vibrations. (Sound being vibrations traveling through a medium, and registering of the vibrations, "hearing.") No matter now minute the someone, or how faint the vibrations, a tree falling will have been heard.

That tree, in the lush forest, *did* make a noise.

Another question: If a rock falls on a distant planet with no life forms, did that rock make a noise?

Taking that question further to the significant question: If something occurs, and is neither registered nor imagined by any life form, did it really occur?

Okay. The question is an oxymoron. Self-contradictory. We are *assuming* that some things did occur, then asking if they really did.

Taking that into account, and *imagining*, say, the rock falling on a distant planet (for on some planets it can be assumed that some rocks do fall)—the question would be regarding that *specific* rock. Did it really fall—AND... *Does it even exist?*—since no life form realizes that it does.

To answer this, one must consider the existence of objects relative to the existence of other objects. If one object is necessary for the existence of another (past, present or future), and it is known *for sure* that one of those objects does exist, then all the others must exist also.

AUGUST 5

Rocks. Rocks! Those hard compactions of minerals found in abundance on planet Earth.
Mountains! A magnificence of rock anchoring valleys and trees and flowers in—
Their place.
Something irrefutable and solid daring to anchor fragility and transience in—
Their place.
A boldness of—boldness itself?
Do rocks anchor time in its place?
Sometimes it feels like it.
Layer upon layer of hardened, compressed—
Time?
Immobilized truths, and history, and mysteries...
Held safeguarded—forever?—in stasis.

AUGUST 6

Onslaughts of heat. Fire!
Lava! Liquified rock—*ROCK!*—so permanent and *solid*—flowing, swirling,
In slow congealment.
Spewing forth! Spewing *UP!* Molten rock—fragmenting and blazing—spewing up—out—
    over—
Beyond.
To think that this can happen to something so solid and stable in our lives. That it can happen to
    foundations.
And since it can, what else might one not be able to count on?
What other foundations of ours might be at risk? Including emotional foundations. And if so, at
    risk from *what?* From
Pressures—fiery pressures!—red-hot passions!—intense desires?
From conflicts, unsettled...
Swirling and spewing!
In heat.

AUGUST 7

Another (of this year's several) fickle questions for you:
What is it like to be a teenager?
(This question is fickle, you know, because *teenagers are fickle*—and also because there are as many answers as there are teens.)

If you are not yet a teenager and are wondering what it will be like to be one, with your hormones all-wacky and in a new life situation—then you possess a healthy outlook and are self-aware. Congrats! You are presently sensible and stable enough (compared to what you will be...), so brace yourself to hang onto your rationality throughout whatever might come. (It might not even be so bad—perhaps pleasurable and exciting as you meet the challenges—but for now, good to be on guard!)

If you *are* a teen, then you know the answer to the question because *this is your life*. You *know* what it's like being a teenager! What you might not know is how to articulate the experience in an objective manner.

Next comes—*ah, yes*—adulthood. Enter objectivity—right? Alas, how quickly one likes to put traumas and unflattering thoughts and experiences behind them. It's more comfortable to look ahead and engage in what's bright and positive—especially while accumulating skills on how to do so. Memories of adolescent years can be selective, out of perspective, and one might even say—*fickle*.

What is it like to be a teenager?
Actually, this very question is presumptuous, because it presumes those who answer it are qualified to speak for others. Since each person's teenage experience is different, one can only answer it for themselves.

AUGUST 8

Fleet of foot and fast of thought.—
Not.
Venturing where one can't be caught.—
Not.
Run little guinea pig!
HIDE!

AUGUST 9

Revenge of the wasp. Make that the revenge of two—three—four—no. Revenge of an *entire squadron* of wasps!

How do they all know to join in? You only thwarted the plans of *one* wasp! Yet here they are, en masse, legs a-dangle, swarming around and down upon you, abuzz with ill intent.

The sting of just one wasp would send the message, but they won't stop there. Oh no! Unlike bees, the same wasp will keep at you in a furious frenzy, stinging you over and over until you finally put an end to it. (Which could well mean putting an end to *the wasp*.)

I know this because throughout childhood I was on the receiving end of that frenzy at least a dozen times. Sometimes on my upper legs while pulling on pants that had been hung out to dry in "the fresh country air," where culprit wasps drop down from a wooden clothespin into the pants.

So we go from a furious pant-trapped wasp to a young child who's none too happy either—angry—and mostly because I'm "not good" if I don't appreciate the carefully laundered and folded clothes tucked "lovingly" into my drawer. *As if that has anything to do with it!*

So now my mother (the laundress) has been drawn into it, having to respond to a stung, having screamed, unappreciative child—her painstakingly calm exterior challenged with an undercurrent of roiling anger. (And *further angry* because it appears she could be perceived as angry, because according to her, she never is.)

And it's possible that the expansion of anger extended further out into the world, to others we encountered throughout the day.

Misunderstandings. Violations of rights. A contagious, volatile spread—in varying degrees—of rage.

Then vengeance?

Is revenge sweet? How readily could it escalate into war?

Is war sweet, satisfying?

And presently, a fervor of intent wasps bearing down *on you*.

Are you one who engages in a venge-fest of war?

AUGUST 10

Why did he (my friend!) set up the situation as win-lose?
Why was he so determined to strike me down?
I wasn't prepared to take him on—no standby stratagems—not in my repertoire for personal relationships.
Thought I could steer him away from win-lose. (Isn't that the humane thing to do? Even if he's no longer a friend, at least he would want to be humane!)
He wouldn't budge. (Why wouldn't he budge?)
So—
I struck *him* down. HARD. I won. But what did I win?
If he'd won, he'd be crowing. High-fiving his buddies. The thought of this is wrenching.
Everything I feel about this is wrenching. Him wanting to hurt me. Me, hurting him.
Whatever victory is, this isn't it.

AUGUST 11

Losses, oh, losses. Too many losses.
Of people. How can a person so real, *so vital,* no longer be in this world??
Of pets. Beloved pets.
Losses of homes. Their warmth, their security.
Of nature's wild places, their affirming familiarity, their *necessity*.
Losses of relationships.
Of dreams.

Voids.
Empty places in one's mind that can be filled with a different kind of vitality: Memories,
        longings, regrets, ruminations…
Or—to let go.
Allowing the losses to slip into, for you—a nothingness.

AUGUST 12

Gains. Gaining! Adding something substantial to your life. To existence.
However small:
      A button sewn back on.
      A dragonfly observed.
      Painting a picture,
      Sealing a letter—sealed with a kiss—
      Greeting someone!
However imaginary:
      Homes that *could* be built.
      Fantasies of adventures to come.
      Reading books,
      Learning!
      Fielding solutions to problems.
Possibilities of what *could be!* Once they occur to you, those thought patterns *EXIST*.
And if you hang onto them, they can keep evolving and enhancing your
Self.

AUGUST 13

Pain. Physical or emotional pain. It—*hurts*. And sometimes it doesn't go away.
Can we assume you want it to go away?
Sometimes people don't. Especially if it's minor pain, it could be so deep in your identity and
    so entwined with how you engage in life, that removing it would take away an essential
    part of you. Such as by carrying around the discomfort of an old war wound, or keeping
    alive how it felt when you nobly suffered through poverty. As reminders—and proof—of
    how you are able to sacrifice.
If so, would you go so far as to revel in the suffering?
Would you scorn others who haven't endured such pain?

In evolutionary terms, pain can be viewed as a wakeup call to attend to something that is wrong.
    So a person *would want* to alleviate it! To counter that, though, pain can also be seen as a
    survival trait in that without alleviation possibilities, those who learn to live with it stay
    alive, and are perhaps valued and admired for doing so.

Or maybe you feel you deserve to be hurting.
But let's say you *don't* want to hurt, and that neither modern nor traditional medicine can relieve
    it. *AND!*—that your friends and those you care about don't want you to hurt.
Would you be willing to look into alleviation possibilities *for them?* Maybe you'll conclude that
    the trouble and expense of accessing care wouldn't be worth the results, or you might
    decide you like your pain's "extra nudge" to keep you alert and hopping—but we're
    talking putting your friends' minds at ease by going to the trouble *to look into it*.
And maybe you'd even be wondering, what kind of a friend is it, anyway, who *wouldn't* want
    you to look into it? Who is okay with seeing you hurting.

AUGUST 14

What if…
You were extraordinarily talented, say a world-class musician. The best of your generation—out of *billions* of people.
You practice, make the most of your inherent talents, and receive accolades.

What if…
You were the same person, with the same musical gifts, but everyone else has identical gifts. That it just evolved as a human characteristic, and regardless of how much you practice, you're nothing special.
You would still be you, as you were born—right?

Now imagine being born with little of a certain trait, say toe dexterity, but everyone else has it—in abundance. And that they have indulged and built a culture around it. They consider their ability an integral and delightful part of being human.
Where would that leave you? Struggling? Looked down upon?
Feeling inferior?
But you're still *YOU!*—with all your assets—regardless of what everyone else is.
Welcome to what it feels like to have a "disability."

AUGUST 15

It is unfortunate the root word of "dementia" is the Latin "demens," meaning loss of mind, and is associated with "demented"—to have lost reason, gone mad. Talk about a word that's laden with negative connotations!
In modern usage "dementia" informally refers to someone losing their memory. It's bad enough to be out an arm or a leg—but can you imagine losing your memories? So much of one's sense-of-self is tied up with memories!
But before going further, an important distinction is to be made. The distinction between "mind" and "memory." Let's call memory an aspect of brain function.
Mind—*whoa!*—this is a category all its own.

Yet losing the brain function of memory is no small thing! Although perhaps it can best be understood by extrapolating from a small thing. We all know what it's like to misplace an item, or to temporarily forget information we once knew, such as a name or, when rushed, the details of specific incidents. Usually the forgotten information will come back to us, because it's all "in there someplace"—right?
Thus it can be said that dementia is simply when one's knowledge remains intact but is increasingly difficult to access.
Whether the information is still "someplace" when one's brain is permanently damaged or one is dead—that's mind territory.

To my loved ones with dementia, this is what I want you to know:
During your lifetime you got many things right, and there were long spans of time when you functioned optimally. Back when you were younger and healthier. That is how I will always remember you—and how I still think of you. Even now when in your company I see your younger self superimposed, simultaneously with, your aging countenance.
In some presently inexplicable way (mind territory) it IS you—and how you will forever remain. Your optimal self.

AUGUST 16

Babies! Babies *galore!*
Each a new life! *Encore! Encore!*
Each—
So pudgy, soft and round.
Gold and pink and black and brown.
Cooing; wailing; asleep like a log.
Charmingly helpless.—

A bundled-up blob?
Could this really be *a person?*
So—*so*—*so*—Yes! Behold each new incarnation
Of whatever a person can be.
Rendering one speechless.
Befuddles in cuddles.
Potentials that complete us.

AUGUST 17

There's gotta be a time and a place for perversity. (No?)
Aren't we are all, each, partly perverse? Defiant!
At times defiant of what's right. Of what's wrong. (Yes! No?)
Sometimes going so far as to defy that there are beginnings and endings? That you once did not exist. That you will die. That you *can* die. Living in the moment.
—But isn't living in the moment how it's done? Throughout each day, whenever focusing on a task or relaxing into a break. So that would be normal. Ignoring death rather than defying it. (Not perverse.)
What about defying someone else's expectation of you? As in, how dare they claim to be thinking *for you!* Perversity there? (Yes?)
What about if you defy their expectation of you those times when you actually happen to agree that it's a good idea? (When if it hadn't been for their interference, it is what you would have done.)
But—*why?* I mean, the whole intent of perversity is to define yourself, for yourself. Right? So why do something to contradict that? Something that negates—yourself.
On the other hand... Are there not times you feel compelled to prove you have a choice and are independent? Possessing free-will is very much who you are!—(Even if you shoot yourself in the foot proving the point?)
Or—how much of it would be because it bugs you when the offender isn't taking other possibilities into account? Possibilities that *you* take into account, and consider as options, but when they don't credit you for having the ability to see more than they do. (The insult of it!)
When *is* the right time—and place—to be perverse?

AUGUST 18

The swimmer dives—
A scene of art!
Grace wherein the waters part,
In descent swift and deep.
Then rising in the same far sweep.
A warm and vibrant dart.—

With velvet water 'gainst her skin,
Bracingly cool, viscously thin.
Purling with each fulsome stroke
Of eager muscles that promote
Calm energy within.

AUGUST 19

The closeness of characteristics between apes and humans can be uncomfortable. Scientists tell us that the DNA sequence of humans and gorillas is 98.3% identical, and of humans and chimpanzees, 98.9% identical.

For those who insist on drawing solid lines of distinction between species—where to draw them?

The similarity of thought processes of chimpanzees and humans is especially striking.

Does this mean our minds are the same?

More: Using apes as the standard, could humans be considered imperfect apes?

Should apes be considered imperfect humans?

Are we close enough in life experiences, cares and concerns, personality traits, physiology, and thoughts to consider ourselves "one"?

To rejoice as one?
To suffer as one?
Or, because of the uncomfortable similarities and potential competitions,
To annihilate one??
...Or the other.

AUGUST 20

Altruism. Selfless concern for the Well-Being of other
Beings.
So they will Be
In a state of wellness—that they value more than their own wellness.

Parents behaving altruistically to benefit their offspring. Dolphins making decisions to prioritize
    other dolphins. Dolphins prioritizing human welfare. Humans sacrificing themselves to
    save other humans—or to save dolphins? Whales sacrificing themselves to help seals.
    Altruism!

It can be seen as an elevated act of friendship for a select individual, or it can be an act to benefit
    random individuals. It can be to benefit groups of
Beings.
It can be an impulsive, fluke act. Or a life pattern.

A way of Beings
Being
Well.

AUGUST 21

Big of size. (Think—*humungous.*)
Strong in love.
A magnanimous whale!
With them, life becomes more leisurely and powerful—
More deep—
Thrusting down, down into depths of free-flowing experience. With ease,
Defying the cumbersomeness of life above.
Deeper—
Weaving in and out amongst themselves. Their bodies weaving, their thoughts weaving, their
    emotions weaving—linking and drawing together the lives they are living. *In-and-out...*
In-and-out...
Until they're they're linking and drawing together *all of living.* Until—
Up to the surface!
And rejoicing—*BIG TIME!*—in their vital equanimity of spirit.

AUGUST 22

How can one misplace a leviathan?
They *were* here,
In all their empty spaces in the ocean.
Rising up in massive dignity,
Mightily exhaling vaporous breath in requisite interludes,
Then inhaling as capacious as their souls are grand,
And plunging back down to their joyous places below.

But where are they now?
What if we were to listen ever-so closely?
Maybe?—Over in that direction? Might that be a whale's enchanting call?
Faint, but *yes*. Listen...
It is a dirge.
A dirge of whales, lost. Plaintive, lonely resonances drifting through the ebbs and currents of the
        deep—
And echoing within
Their own vacant spaces.

AUGUST 23

Look! Up in the sky! It's a bird! It's a plane! It's a—*bicycle?* With wings?
Of all unprecedented marvels—what could possibly come next? Bi-planes doing loop-de-loops? Dare-devils standing upright upon the wings, clothes whipping frenziedly—as if to be torn from their (*ooo...*) muscular bodies?
Goggled aviators crossing the continents?—Crossing the vast, restless oceans? *Encircling* the world?
After having been Earth-bound since back... back... to the furthest reaches of human evolution... back to the furtherest reaches of our fantasizing of flying... for flying to have now become reality!
An unshackling from gravity, heaviness, burdens. An uplifting of the heart!
Rockets piercing Earth's atmosphere into space. *Exploring space!* Astronauts. Captain Kirk. Klingons. Collectively doing loop-de-loops *among the stars!*—weaving together celestial realities and our fantasies.
Ever inspiring! Ever youthful it is, to inspire. Ever brazen.
The daring young men in their flying machines!

AUGUST 24

How to keep the awesome, handsome, masculine onlookers from knowing I'm embarrassed?
If they know I'm embarrassed, that would be even more embarrassing.
Must be cool and collected—yes—as if I'm not warm and blushing.
As if the original—umm, "trifling"—didn't happen.
But isn't this blushing a dead giveaway?
So now they know that I know (more blushing...)
That they know (even redder...)—(*Will this never stop getting worse?*)
(Redder... redder...)
Oh, shit.

AUGUST 25

Those who believe they are perfect by virtue of never having made a mistake are under pressure to get everything right—the first time.

Maybe they do get a lot right when under such pressure, but it is *impossible* to get e*verything* absolutely—unequivocally—*always* right. Even babies make mistakes, and toddlers for sure, as they delve intrepidly into their lives. Walking too fast (and falling!), screaming or hitting out when they want an object (when all they'd have to do is carefully reach and grab it), sitting passively and *nothing* happens. It's how they learn and grow! It's disconcerting that some folks live in denial that *they* ever made a mistake.

Even when it's obvious to everyone else they've made a mistake, there they are twisting facts around, and sometimes even changing their life course so it "appears" they are perfect. "Look! No errors here!"

Right. And it maintains their feeling of superiority over everyone else.

Right. And sometimes they're seething mad about it, too. About "having had to" shift their life around. Blaming others for the trouble of it.

So. If these individuals are resistant to learning and growing, is there some way the rest of us can learn to optimally live with them?

It being particularly difficult when such confident (and disrespectful) persons are in positions of power.

AUGUST 26

It has been said that the road to Hell is paved with good intentions.
It is also said that no good deed goes unpunished.

What do you think of those proverbs? Drawing from your own experiences regarding good intentions gone awry, would you like to take a crack at coming up with your own proverb?
If so, imagine a time when you meant well but the results went so haywire that it would have been better had you left matters alone. Hadn't done anything!—
Or better yet, picture a time when someone messed *you* up, when you know (or assume) they are a basically good person.

Okay. Ready? (Maybe have a sheet of paper and pen handy…)
One way to begin formulating your proverb would be to call out the offender by name or pseudonym, such as "The time Karla covered for me on my shift without telling me first, and got me fired by throwing out the boss's lucky rag."
In that scenario your words-of-wisdom might be: "Karla's obsession with cleaning does away with good luck." Or, "Cleaning up doesn't always make life cleaner."

(Got one? Take your time.)
Next, consider your feelings toward the person who mistreated you. Do you believe what they did *really was* an oversight, a mistake?
Have you forgiven them?
The final question: If something major good were to come from the mishap, would that absolve them from what they did?

AUGUST 27

The answer first: *Surely not!*
The question: Is life nothing but a big joke the multiverse is playing on us?

If someone is in on a joke, then they are not the butt of it.
So if life is a joke, let's be in on it!
But what can be funny about *being alive*—about existence? For one, without doubt I know *your* existence is to be taken seriously.

On the other hand… Can not too much seriousness become constricting? When life closes in too tight and confusing and painful—when one could sure use a break. A good hearty laugh now and then?
And the more intense your conundrums, then the more relieving it is to break into a laugh! The matching intensity of each experience resulting in a balancing of sorts?

On the *other* other hand… When there's *not enough* seriousness in one's life—when everything is taken too lightly—then breaking into laughter has little to balance out. The person gets lopsided into superficiality, and laughing becomes a mockery of what others value and enjoy.

Lest we forget what some consider to be the biggest joke the multiverse might be playing on us. What they consider the ultimate wrong. Death. (*da-dummm…*) To have life (to them, the ultimate right) and then for it to be—*gone*.

Is there really a semblance of life—and death—as being "a big joke"?

AUGUST 28

Serenity is a lake
Lying flat and far,
Bestirred gently by wind and the occasional supple dip of your oars, or by the tottering cleave of
        the bow of your boat.—
A boat hewn soundly. You know it to be trustworthy.
You row freely to port, or to starboard. Wherever you will to be—will be—where you are.
Where you *should be.*
The grievousness of life's problems are—somewhere. Somewhere—off—where *they* should be.
Not here.
Everything in existence is where it should be.
The far, flat lake—as is, where it should be. The hat cocked on your head—just so. As it should
        be. Your tackle box, your lunch, your feet stable and firm on the floorboard.
All, being right—and existing in lake-time. Which is not suspended moments of time, or time-
        out-of-time,
But a standard of time.
A time when sun shines warm and insets buzz and distant hills
Keep their distance.
With lures trailing and floats bobbing idly,
The air tinged with subtle scents,
And yesterday's dreams slapping duly against wooden sides of trust.

AUGUST 29

Nessie! Nessie! Come to me!
You of folklore and fancy and fame.
Show me your sinuous curves and enigmatic personality.
I love you—I promise.
It's not every day I get to picnic on the banks of your renowned Highland peek-out-hole lake,
    which might possibly be lying fathoms above dark oceanic crevices, beneath. Is deep
    below—or somewhere off beyond the deep below?—where you cavort and call home?
Where are you??
I will not think less of you for having met you. Your mysterious aura will not dispel! As with all
    nature, the more I know of someone, the more their mystery deepens.
I promise.
But I know—I know—just because you're special to me doesn't mean I'm special to you.
And the friend I bring you thinks we've been here long enough and that better pastimes await
    back at our inn.
But he doesn't know—*and don't you know?*—that to make your acquaintance is *far better*
    because it would bind the three of us in this one-of-a-kind moment.
How much longer, Nessie? (*Oh, Nessie.*)

And how much longer must so many others, the world-round, keep waiting for their intrigues to
    pan out?

AUGUST 30

Good morning, class! Welcome to Chipmunk Childcare. I am Ms. Linda. I will be your teacher.
Today is August 30th. This is a calendar, and this 30, in this box here, represents today. A three
 and a zero—for thirty. Every day, at nine o'clock, we will start class. This is a clock. The
 short hand will be pointing at nine. The long hand at twelve. We start class with calendar
 time and finger plays.
We have already had free play for those who got here early. If you come early, you can have
 breakfast here. It is always the same breakfast: Yogurt, oatmeal, and fruit. Lunch will be
 many different things! Everyone gets lunch at Chipmunk Childcare!
On Tuesdays we will go on a field trip to the grocery store and pick out lunches for the coming
 week. There are also many fruits and vegetables growing in the backyard. You can pick
 these to snack on whenever you like, and eat as much as you like. In Spring we will plant
 more vegetables. And flowers!
Alex—yes?—if you have a question please raise your hand. Yes, that is your name on
 September's calendar—this is September's calendar—in box 15. And the letters after
 your name, D-A-D spell "Dad" On the 15th of September it is your father's birthday.
 You will get to make something special for him on that day.
Louis? Oh, yes, what a good idea! Maybe we will do that later today.

...Are your fingers still tingling and twitchy from bending them so funny? Now it is art time.
 After calendar time and finger plays, it is art time. Today you get to make a booklet, titled
 "All About Me." Here is the first page. It is an outline of a person. What you do is use
 crayons to color in hair and a face, and on the body draw clothes to make the person look
 just like you! If your hair is brown use a brown crayon to draw your hair. If your eyes are
 blue, use a blue crayon. Then look at your clothes and see if you can draw them on the
 person. There is a mirror on the wall, here, you can look in.

Yes, Louis? No, your picture doesn't have to look *exactly* like you. You are making a drawing to represent you. And don't worry if you color outside the lines. That's okay. Just try to pick the right colors.

While you're coloring, I will come around to each of you to fill in the blanks on page two. The blanks are for your name, your age, your favorite color, your favorite food, and what you like doing most.

No, Louis, you don't have to write anything. Tell me what you want to say, and I will write it for you. Then everyone in your family who can read, can read your book! And some day, when you are in big-kid school, you will learn how to read and you can read your book, too!

Yes, Isabelle, you can start coloring now.

I can't wait to learn all about you!

AUGUST 31

...Now jump up and down three times, spin around waving your arms, and settle into your chair for art.

Today's art project is a paper collage. Here are two example collages to show you what we're doing. This is our bin of scrap paper, and you will each get a pair of scissors. If you have never used scissors before, I will show you how, or if I'm busy helping someone else, maybe a classmate will show you. Clara knows how—and you, too, Isabelle?

With the scissors you cut out different shapes from the scrap paper. When you have enough shapes, give the scissors back to me, and I will hand you a large sheet of manilla paper and a glue stick. Then you glue down your colored shapes wherever you would like them to be on the large manilla paper. You can make an abstract design—like this example—or you can make a picture out of them—like this house and tree.

Yes, Isabelle, there are stickers on one of the pictures! After you glue down your paper shapes, if you like, you can pick out up to five stickers from the sticker bin to add to your collage. Do you like the little squirrels on the tree and the bug in the house? There are lots of different stickers to choose from!

...Yes, Rory, we are headed back now. Did you notice we are walking in a large square? You did!

Do you have many things in your nature bags? *Ooooh—yes—*what a cool pinecone! And the twisty seedpods! We'll ask Anthony's mom what kind of trees these are from. And Alex—so many rocks! We have a rock book back at school that tells all about them.

What did you think of *Peter Rabbit* yesterday? He was a pretty naughty little rabbit, wasn't he? Today's story will be another Beatrix Potter story about another animal having adventures. No, I'm not going to tell you what story. It will be a surprise. What? Louis? You already know? Yes, that's it! It's the book on the top of the magazine rack next to

the bookshelf. You have only been in school one day, and you figured that out already!
Once every month we will go on a field trip to the library, and you will each get to pick out one book that I will read at story time. Do you remember when story time is? Yes! It is right after lunch.
Here, let me take Tussock's leash now. He's pulling because he's so close to home.

SEPTEMBER

SEPTEMBER 1

The eastern continental shelf stretches wide... to a distant north,
And wide to a distant south,
Underlying forceful, warm oceanic currents. Upon which long miles of horizontal waves roll in and lap the shoreline. Low waves.
Looking out beyond the incoming waves, one can see that further east they are parallel with a swath of darker, deeper ocean—
Which is hugged, still *farther out,* by a thick lo-oong cap of rolling fog.
Then FARTHER EAST...
Almost beyond imagination... lies a distance where repetitively, day upon day, the sun rises. The eastern horizon.
It takes some courage to look in that direction. The sun already having risen. As if in that direction lies—the past. That which has already happened. Histories.
A direction from which came ships. And conquering civilizations. And wondrous innovative ideas. And diseases—and destruction. And beloved ancestors.
—And lamenting—oh, lamentations—of all that went wrong and didn't have to be.
A wide, distant reminder of the irrevocable.
And of
Acceptance.

SEPTEMBER 2

Swishing and swooshing with splashes that chime,
The dolphins are playing concerto maritime.
Lyrically leaping in unison fine,
The dolphins are keeping their humor in line.
Splashes that chime.
Swishing and swooshings of sleek, nimble spine.
Lyrically leaping,
Concertedly keeping
The gist of their jestful pastime.

SEPTEMBER 3

Vanity? Vanity!
For those of Christian faith, please reference your Bible, Ecclesiastes 3:19:

"For that which befalleth the sons of men befalleth beasts; even one thing befallenth them: as the one dieth, so dieth the other; yea, they have all one breath; so that a man hath no preeminence above a beast: for all is vanity."

SEPTEMBER 4

Ahimsa. The ancient Hindu, Buddhist, and Jainist principle of non-violence and compassion toward all living beings.
Reverence for life.
A time-honored outlook that quells an inner restlessness. A way to put one's life into perspective.
A way to envision that helping one, helps the all.
That debasing one, debases the all.
Filling in the gaps of what one doesn't understand with trust.
Trust in Ahimsa.
Always risky to trust. Alway prices to pay.—
But with Ahimsa to believe that the goal of reverence for life is worth any risks involved.

With reverence for those who so rever.

SEPTEMBER 5

sssweee-PT! PT!
Sudden blasts of wind on an unsettled, overcast, wind-stirred day. Hits! Wind hits on bushes,
      houses, trees—animals. The animals feeling menaced. Attacked.
Sudden bursts of blood through the body, hitting arteries. Hitting the brain! Instant certainty of—
Danger!
But danger from what?
Alarmed quail break instantaneously from their hidden ambulations, launching themselves—up!
      Becoming cloudy masses of percussive, airborne wings. Stirring amid the already
      stirring, dark clouds.
A single rousted rabbit dashes hither—thither—then—*oh! oh! where to go??*
Smacks of base pressure, and feeling pressured—
To do *what?*

SEPTEMBER 6

Who are the spacelings—and how dare they buzz our beloved Earth?

Earth is *ours*, all of us who live here and who evolved here. Who among us gave them permission to fly by?—not to mention possibly land or otherwise meddle!

Who are they?

Just because they are technologically superior, do they think Earth is theirs?

Yet... Do not some earthlings claim ownership of other of Earth's creatures? It is one of the attitudes that has occurred throughout the history of humankind. Some humans even claim to own *other humans*, and proceed (shamelessly) to exploit them. If that's how life works, who are we to complain when other beings might try to get away with doing the same to us?

If that's what the spacelings are up to. *Are* they staking out the place? Weighing the pros and cons of using Earth and its life to their advantage?

The outrage is that they are in a position to consider it. It puts us at their mercy. Would you like to be at the mercy of someone you know nothing about?

Who ARE they??

They're not helping us out here by meeting us partway. No friendship overtures. No respect for our input. If they were to open up a little to us, then *we* could decide whether, and how much, to share *our* planet with them. Each helping the other out.

On the other hand...

Since they've been keeping tabs on us, why should they respect us? If we desire the friendship of alien beings, it seems the best way—*the only way*—is to make ourselves worthy of their respect—and worthy of their trust.

To behave in manner that earns it.

So far the spacelings have shown a tolerance of us. Perhaps they're even hoping we'll get our act together so we *can* be friends.

SEPTEMBER 7

"My Pet Chicken," by Roger, age 7.

My pet chicken is named Francie. She thinks I'm her mother. I saw Francie hatch! She was wet and skinny, and then she dried off and got fluffy.

Francie likes Grape Nuts and fat worms. She likes it when I pet her. I like to make Francie happy! She follows me around like I'm her mother. When I'm sad Francie makes me feel better. She is the only one who understands me.

Francie is my best friend.

SEPTEMBER 8

Modern culture is increasingly accepting of both physical and mental "disabilities," and increasingly provides services without maligning or stigmatizing the individual. Those with autism, for example, or Down syndrome, can now readily be seen as variations of what humans are—not something apart and to be feared.
Confusion and fear, however, still surround those with "antisocial personality order"—who are frequently denounced as "sociopaths" or "psychopaths."
Imagine being slapped with one of those labels!
The following is a primer to help sort through the confusion:

Depending what study you read, anywhere from 1% to 25% of the human population are sociopaths. 25% would mean, on average, one out of every four people you encounter is a sociopath.
Clarification is called for. If 1% of people have antisocial personality disorder (ASPD), that would be the for-sure psychopaths. A looser definition of ASPD would include a spectrum of individuals with low empathy ability, embracing about 25% of humans.
But who is qualified to draw the line at 25% and say that those above that benchmark are "normal" and those below it are "sociopaths?" *Everyone* has a different degree of empathetic ability, so we are *all* somewhere on the spectrum of 0%-100% ability.
How we each adapt to wherever we fall on the spectrum would be a better criterion for being labeled sociopathic. For example, someone with low ability, at, say 10% ability, may have adapted well and be high-functioning, with great friendships and well-suited employment. No problem, no label. But someone up in the 25% range—or higher—may be struggling and unhappy with their low ability. To classify that person in the "sociopathic range" would gain them access to psychiatric services to help them function well and happily.—

But it would also slap them with that derisive and crippling label of "sociopath."

Consider that 25% or so of the population is *a lot* of people to have low empathy ability! This would include *our children,* our friends, our family. Those we love! Most of them well-meaning, trying hard, overcoming obstacles and enduring various levels of hurt—in order to become the successful people they want to be. Our neighbors. Our work associates.

It *might* be true that the lowest 1%—the psychopaths—are incapable of loving and compassion, but the rest are not. They interact with the world differently than highly empathetic folks, but are capable of great caring, love, loyalty—and are often extraordinarily dutiful. "Sociopath" is not a dirty word.

SEPTEMBER 9

Whippity-flippity. How can it do that?
A *snake!* Flipping up a tree!
In a rippy-zippy flying spree.
      Slashing the air.
        Thrashing with flair
To uppermost branches. Taking wild chances.
For what? Just 'cuz it's there??

SEPTEMBER 10

Snagged!
Caught off-guard by someone—or *something*—and you find yourself in over your head.
Perhaps having committed to organizing a charity yard sale, but obstacles and distractions keep interfering.—
Or you said you'd help construct a new lean-to. They're counting on you! But you're not as skillful as you'd off-handedly been boasting, and everyone is sure to be disappointed.
Or what if you led someone to believe you're in love with them and can be trusted. Not true?—
Snagged!
How to redeem oneself when riddled with anxiety, dread—self-doubt? You *meant to* do all these things. You *know* you're a good person. Yet—where's the evidence? You're vulnerable. Exposed—and open. But open to what? To being hurt? Open to new possibilities Especially when caught in the love affair snag (the most egregious snag),
Where being vulnerable and open is...
Confoundedly—fortuitously?—the precise, *exact* state of mind when one—how can this be happening?—*when one falls in love.*
So—nothing else for it. Why not? And you may find (again—*how can this be happening?*)— you may find...
It's wonderful being in love!
You pull your act together and the lean-to turns out acceptable enough. "Thanks for doing the yard sale" they all say. *Whew!*
Scraped by *this time.*

SEPTEMBER 11

Wisemen have been known to warn: "We create that which we fear." If so—something worth knowing?
Imagine, for example, abhorring *even the thought* of spiders to the point that you deny their existence. Spiders being so incongruous with your notion of a just, right world—or with a life worth living—that they *can't* exist.
So if there are no spiders, then there's no need to put out peppermint oil or any other deterrent. You are neither on-guard for them, nor have a plan of action for if you were to encounter one.
Then when confronted with a spider dangling from the ceiling—*horror!*—yet it can be said you created this very situation. Set yourself up for it.
People can live in denial of any number of unpleasant realities, living in "blissful ignorance"—until...?

Next, imagine a child being told by someone they believe, "No good person would want to damage that sofa." (*Actually—the child would love to jump all over it, maybe cut it open to see what the stuffing looks like.*) Or, "You don't want to touch that." (*The child does.*) Or, "Only reprehensible people would want to have sex with that floozy." (*Hey, fantasies are fantasies.*)
Imagine this child growing up with repressed fears of who, deep-down, they really are.
Then... "Freudian slips" start happening. They wear gem-studded pants on a sofa, cutting it up—then gush forth with apologies, can't believe they did it. (*But can't shake the "knowledge" it is who they are.*) There's a type of honesty going on here, and likewise when they "just happen" to handle and break forbidden objects, or copulate with whomever they like, or...?

Would this be the parent's or teacher's fears having come true? *The child's* deep fears having
   come true?
What will be the now-grown child's self-image?
...Having created that which they feared.

SEPTEMBER 12

Imagine a crystal ball for today's verse.
And a fortune teller. Her hands sweep felicitously around the ball's gleaming contour, focusing her sight within, coaxing the spirits to conjoin. Crooning to them.
Madam V'doma is garbed in layered complexities of color, texture, scarfery, earrings, bangles—tiny reflected glints, piddling little shadows—
While her crystalline ball encloses layers and complexities of realms. Depths in curvatures. Contortions. Multiple foci into—
She starts! Her eyes widen as the orb shifts from a brief clarity into swirling, stormy darkness. Madam V'doma looks up at you, locking eyes, and in low, measured tones relays—

"You have a warning. You are vulnerable. *BEWARE!* Beware to whom you become beholden.
Beware the schmoozer—you know of whom I speak.
Beware of over-committing yourself to him.
You will be forced to choose between what you think is honor and what you know to be right. But you do not know the deep-within-deep meaning of honor."
She narrows her eyes, skewering you: "Seek out the true meaning of honor!"

You experience a thudding disorientation as the ball fades to empty. A menacing music you hadn't been aware was playing ceases. Had the music only been in your head? And wasn't that a putrid stench? Your nasal passages smart as if there had been one.
Madam V'doma gathers up her skirts and turns aside, rising. Enough of this! (Enough of *you!*) When—

Her crystal ball jolts back to life with a bright, heralding *twing!*

This has never happened before. She is taken aback. Doesn't like it. Mutters "Ce este asta?" as she settles back into her chair and half-curious, half-desultory, turns her attention back into the ball.
"It seems the spirits have another message for you." She snarled it. "It seems you did not—will *in the future* not—take the advice of the orb. You will not know honor. *YOU WILL MAKE THE WRONG CHOICE.*" She looks up at you with sharp disapproval. You are beneath her, and certainly beneath this special attention of the orb, which now swirls merrily with pastels and sparkles.—
It never did this for *her*, she of integrity, and respectful and loyal to the spirits, all these years. Yet, because she prides herself that *she* knows honor, Madam V'doma bites back jealousy.and continues to relay truthfully to you the message:
"You will make the wrong choice. There will be suffering, and you will pay. You will know. But something unforeseen, and what the spirits consider—delightful—will come of it all.
They do not tell me what." The fortune teller's dark eyes now soften a little—just a little, perhaps in wonderment—as she finishes. "The orb," she pauses, pursing her lips. "The orb—
Laughs."

SEPTEMBER 13

Personal adornments. To enhance how you look?
Lovely, delicate earrings? Bold flashy earrings? Nose-rings?—
Necklaces? Bracelets?—
NO jewelry?
Make-up??
Your—*oh so personal*—choice of clothing and clothing accessories.
So others can see you how you wish to be seen? Or—
So you can feel good about yourself, whether or not others see you? To feel comfortable within your life. Within yourself.
To send messages!
To have FUN!
To openly and trustingly share yourself and your personality with the world!
...Or to hide? Or deceptively mislead.
To tantalizingly—teasingly—conceal select aspects of yourself from others?
Any one of which, enhancing far more than your physical body. Adornments—or lack thereof—enhancing your personality! Who you are!

SEPTEMBER 14

Is everyone awake from nap now? Rory? Anthony?—you sure slept a long time today!
For today's game, everyone needs to make a big circle, then sit down on the grass. That's right.
      Rory—skooch in a little closer. That's good.
It's time for... *Duck Duck Goose!* Do you remember how to play? That's right. Clara will start
      out, walking around behind everyone, tapping each of you lightly on the head and
      declaring you either a duck or a goose. If you are a duck, stay where you are. If you're a
      goose, you get up and chase Clara around the circle, trying to tag her before she gets
      safely to your spot. If you tag her before she gets there, she has to sit in the center, and
      you are "it."
Okay Clara. Are you ready?

Isabelle? Alex?—Clara. Are you still playing *Duck Duck Goose?* Oh—*Fox Fox Chicken*—I see.
      And when the fox catches the chicken—he *eats it?* Oh, my! I see. (*giggle giggle*)
Rory, the tree branches are still a little wet and slippery from the sprinklers. This isn't a good
      time to climb it.—LOUIS! ANTHONY! What's going on? You know the rules, Louis.
      You only play a war game when the other person wants to play, too, and when you both
      agree on the rules. *It is a game.* Any time the other person wants to stop, *THEN THE
      GAME IS OVER*. Did you tell Louis you wanted to stop, Anthony? You did? Then
      STOP! Louis.

SEPTEMBER 15

A woodland song of emotions.
For one or more voices to sing in unison. The emotions—

A disappointment. A hungry weasel that didn't catch its prey: *urrrrumph urrrrumph*
A triumphant coyote: *arrooOOO! arrooOOO!*
The cheerful glottal hum of a badger moseying about its business: *krrrup krrrrrrup krrup*

(Practice) *krrrup krrup krrup krrup — urrrumph urrrumph urrumph — krrrrrrrup! — arrooOOO! arrooOOO!*

More sounds—

The high-pitch of air through feathers of a diving predatory bird: *shrrrrrrrr*
Trees, bushes: *wooooooo—kak—shhhhh*
Insects: *bzzzzzzzzz*
A downed squirrel: *EEEEEch!*
The soft undulating breath of a contented sleeping elk: *puhhh puhhh*

Feel the emotions? (It takes a while. That's okay.) A little more practice?
Ready to sing? Here we go—

puhhh puhhh puhhhhh puh! puhhh puhhh — wooooo wooooo — krrrup krrrup krrrup — shrrrrrrrrrrr — EEEEEch! — kak kak wooo woooooo — shhhhhh! shhhhhhh — puhhh puhhh puhhh puhhh — shhhhhhhh — bzzzzzzzzz — woooooo — krrrup krrup krrrrrp — puhhh puhhh — woooo wooooo wooooooooo — urrrumph — kak! — arrooOOO! arrooOOOOO!

bzzzzzzzzz

SEPTEMBER 16

There are multiple ways of evaluating a religion, pro and con, but here is perhaps a new method:
That it not be about whether to endorse the ideology or beliefs of a particular faith, or whether to become a member, but rather about whether to be *a friend* of it.
To evaluate in this manner, look around at those practicing the religion and see if there's anyone you admire exceedingly—and if they claim to be the way they are *because* of their faith. This is the connection to look for! Then you would be a friend of the religion in the same manner that a good friend of a good friend is likewise, your friend.
—Thus rendering it a friendship issue, rather than a theology issue.
And to hone your religion evaluation skills would mean honing your skills on how to best evaluate people. With close attention to what it is you admire in people, and why.
Then!...*After* you are a friend of assorted religions, and if you are of mind to join one, decide which one you feel most comfortable with—and go along with whatever brand of spirituality they offer up. All spiritual beliefs having some plusses. (And some minuses.)

SEPTEMBER 17

Peering out through crisp green leaves and gnarled branches of brushwood.
It takes but one narrow slit of an opening to see out, or just a pinhole opening, while you crouch down, obscured by a diversity of colors, shapes, shadows, light. Seeing, but unseen.
Motionless. Hearing, but unheard.
Downwind. Smelling, but not smelled.
Thinking, but not thought of. Calculating, considering, feeling…
Caring. Understanding.
To exist!—
As if you don't exist. Spying upon life's matrix of mystery—
While making yourself part of the mystery.

SEPTEMBER 18

Security run amuck.
How can they think nothing will ever go wrong?
Like children begging their parents to let them wakeboard, when they are too slight and weak to manage the board. Or they oh-so-confidently believe they can bungee jump, or pilot the motorboat, or whatever else seems like *a great!* idea.
If their parents say it's okay, then surely it has to be safe! Nothing bad will happen to them.
Pushing against their parents, to get what they want.
Pushing their limits, as if they had no limits. (Can invincibility have limits?)
Eating all the candy they can get away with eating, secure their teeth will never rot. No pain in store! Or if their teeth do rot out, something to compensate, or better, will replace them.
Not unlike cartoon characters splatting and dying—then popping right back up again, free to override death in continually exciting ways.
And if there *ever is pain*, then that's just the way it is. Can't be helped. Just scream out in protest —or stoically accept "God's will."

Except... That's not "just the way it is."
Children get to grow up!

...Or do they? Can you not see a similarity between children trying to get away with everything they can, and adults pushing the limits of the authority in their lives—including their political system? Confident that in the U.S.A. nothing fundamentally bad will happen to the system. That it can't! Or if it does, something just as good or better will pop back up in its place.

Faith in the security that their rights and freedoms, will always be their rights and freedoms.
As if democracy could never break.
As if they aren't the ones—if they aren't careful—with the potential to break it.

SEPTEMBER 19

Timelines provide reference points that help one organize historical events. The chronology is divided into B.C.E. (before common era) and C.E. (common era). Events have a date such as "Babylon fell in 539 B.C.E." Or, "in 1969 C.E. Apollo 11 landed on the moon with three astronauts aboard." (You will also come across the more familiar denotations of B.C. and A.D.) The center point of 0 represents the year Christ was born—everything happening before then counting back into B.C.E., and everything coming after counting forward into C.E. (starting with year 1).

Your personal-life timeline is a world apart! Most folks count their birth as point 0, and chronologically consider events to be happening "when I was 5 years old" or 25 years old, or whenever.

Except... if something acutely traumatic were to happen in their life—so-much-so that they feel like a different person before that date, then after that date. An acute trauma might be if a bomb detonated on your hometown and you were forced to emigrate, your prior life in shambles. Or if your fundamental support system fails you—or a particular person fails you—catching you so off-guard you are unprepared—*or unable*—to navigate the new life you find yourself cast into.

Another example: Although others may think your life is going well, you can't see beyond a certain date, such as after graduation, or post-marriage. Your imagination drawing a blank when trying to reach out beyond then.

In those cases, henceforth, your reckoning of time will consider everything happening after then as A.T. (after the trauma) or B.T. (before your trauma).

The question: Would it be your fault you were unprepared?

SEPTEMBER 20

Remember Madam V'doma? She who foretells the future, and has issued warning to beware to whom one becomes beholden? Do you consider that good advice? You take your chances when accepting favors or compliments from someone, for then you'll feel an indebtedness to them—perhaps even slipping into feeling loyalty to them.
Depending how much the gift-giver disrespects and disregards you, they may call in those debts with injurious consequences for you.
Nevertheless, it's your decision to make. As an adult. But here is her advice as regards your children:

"Be careful to whom you allow your children to become beholden."
From whom you allow them to accept favors, gifts, help.
Because when they come of age they may feel a loyalty to people or institutions, which agonizes them. Loyalties they would not have entered into, had it been their adult decision, but now they may feel honor-bound to those involved, to follow through with what you have set in motion for them. Except, now, it would be *themselves* choosing to do so.—
Against their better judgment,
And *themselves* paying whatever prices are to be paid for it.

SEPTEMBER 21

Have another mushroom, Bro.
Shove aside. Thanks.
Have a good snuffle in this damp, sun-pierced copse.
Ahhh...
Decaying earth. Adept, diggin', heavy hooves.
Ahhh...
You there, Ma?
We're a family. We're bristly. We're content.

Have a javelina
Day!

SEPTEMBER 22

Don't ask me to have pity on you. Whoever you are, and whatever situation you're in, I'm doing you a favor by not complying with your request.
I would think you were selling yourself short by asking. (You can do better!)
If you are hurt or suffering through no fault of your own, I am sad on your behalf, and I may reach out to you in sympathy. I would do so *on my own*.

To appeal for mercy from someone is different. If they are in a position to wrong you—or are engaged in wronging you—then you deserve their mercy, and depending upon the situation, you might want to try asking for it. You would be asking for a behavior, and the request would come from a position of strength. Because you are right.
Whereas asking for pity comes from a position of weakness. As if you believe you are entitled to someone's sympathy. It would be *an emotion* you were requesting—and everyone gets to feel whatever it is they feel.
Moreover, it can be demoralizing when folks pity. Sometimes they feel superior that the misfortune is yours, not theirs. They might feel helpless in that, not wanting to feel superior. Or they might be angry about it. Or revel in their superiority!
Not much you can do about *whatever* others are feeling towards you. Speculating on what it might be can be unpleasant. Humiliating.
So why tempt people to respond with denigrating emotions—by asking for their pity?

SEPTEMBER 23

You deserve better than to be lied to.
Whenever an important decision is to be made that affects your life or the lives of those you care about, then accurate information enables you to achieve the outcome you want.
When someone feeds you a lie, they deny you this power. They don't care if you do something you wouldn't want to do.
It is disrespectful! It is controlling. Manipulative.

When it happens in your personal life, you become a fool. But the liars are not the ones who make you a fool. It is you, for having believed them.
This can be hard to swallow, that the fault is yours, but necessary in order to recover and be willing to trust again.

One of the most unfair things that can happen to an individual is if they die in the midst of being a fool, having never caught on that they are. Then they would never have the earthly opportunity to recover, to learn from their mistake—and to become the person they want to be.

SEPTEMBER 24

The elusive Bird of Happiness...
And what a beauty! Let's see if we can figure her out.
Waxing lyrical would be fun, but how about a scientific approach today? To supplement verse with the support of research studies, statistics, analyses... To fence our bird in long enough to take a good look at her.

A common tendency among those studying happiness is to correlate it with success. In order for their conclusions to be valid, however, both "happiness" and "success" must be defined. What is meant by "happiness"? By "success"?
Towards defining happiness:
For decades polls have repeatedly ranked Finland, Denmark and Sweden in the top "happiest countries on Earth." Only recently have segments of the scientific community come to doubt these results. Turns out these northern European countries are among those with the highest rates of per capita depression and suicide. So how, they contend, could the people living there be the happiest?
One possibility is that those conducting the polls are equating "happiness" with "contentment" —so maybe these folks are the most content with their lot in life.
Would you agree that happiness and contentment are the same thing?
Or could it be these Northern Europeans *enjoy* their trademark "gloominess"?
Another possibility: They are not content so much as "complacent" in that they feel little responsibility for anyone other than themselves. As long as they each perform a minimum of "duty"—hey—they're good.

There is actually some evidence for that last possibility. In 2022 Peter Zashev, PhD, wrote in the *Helsinki Times*: "Stoicism makes us unfeeling… we are not that interested in one another and have little tolerance for people who may share their frustrations, difficulties, or unhappiness." He is talking about not valuing empathy—and there can be relief in "not having to bother" empathizing. Might that attitude translate into complacency?

Then Dr. Zashev goes on to point out that over half of all Finns take antidepressants. So could it be that being drugged is lulling them into feeling happy?

Or—perhaps because Finns, in their depression, might be awash in low expectations—and as such, any little good thing that comes their way could incline them to claim happiness?

They also seem bent on confusing having "dutiful social bonds" with what empathy is all about. Are they a country with a high ratio of sociopaths, and have accepted that as the norm?

When analyzing scientific studies, in addition to keeping an eye on the terminology, one should also bear in mind that any individual within a large group of people, such as a country, may be quite different than the majority around them. (Just because someone is a Finn, for example, doesn't automatically mean they're depressed!)

Towards defining success:

Be especially wary what is meant by this word! In highly competitive societies it is easily assumed that "achieving" high social status and material wealth well above basic needs is the epitome of success. Yet time-and-time-again studies have shown that having such success does not ensure happiness.

Then what about "power"? How does being powerful enter into a person's state of happiness? Would you say it is an essential component of happiness?

Keep in mind there are two primary ways to define "power." One: Having control over others, and over the way of the world. Two: Having control over oneself.

Regarding number two: Yes. Polls repeatedly indicate that those who feel in control of themselves and feel responsible for themselves are basically happy. (Including being vouched for by our Northern European academic, Dr. Zashev.)

Regarding number one: Too many variables, depending on definitions. No definitive study linking having power over others with happiness.

To address the nuances of "success": Would you consider yourself a success if you were to reach *your own goals* that you set for yourself?—other than the goals of great riches, status, or power. However modest your goals may be, if they are something you value and you would like others to see you in that light, would you feel successful upon having achieved them?

Would you be *happy?*

Or does your personal feeling of happiness come more from enjoying the journey along the way than actually reaching a goal?

All of the preceding commentary having been preliminary, to rev up your brain synapses to best interpret the statistics. Now—a sampling of the statistics!

- According to Eric Baker in his book *Plays Well With Others* (2022), people with five or more friends with whom they talk and confide are 60% happier than those with a lesser number of friends.

- Meanwhile, Robert Waldinger, M.D., renowned Harvard researcher in the science of happiness, has clarified that one doesn't need to have multiple friends to be happy, that just one or two good friends can be enough. (This per the extensive, on-going Harvard happiness study which commenced in 1938, and involves numerous participants.)

- From the National Bureau of Economic Research: "If you consider your spouse to be your best friend you are twice as happy as those who don't."

- Psychologist Edward E. Diener, a.k.a. "Dr Happiness", said people are happy if they think they are happy. (This is called "subjective well being.")

- Studies abound linking happiness with patterns of generosity—not only according to polls, but according to hardcore research, such as by neuroscientist Phillippe N. Tobler, University of Zurich, Switzerland, who studied neural brain links documenting this phenomenon. Dr. Tobler concludes, "Helping others and being generous to them increases happiness."

(This is good stuff! It keeps adding to the accumulated knowledge of humankind!)

- Now, oh gosh—where to begin?—regarding the overwhelming research, polls, anecdotal observations—not to mention your probable own experiences—connecting happiness with gratitude.

To cite just one study, also from across-the-pond (University of Leicester, U.K.), psychologists Alex M. Wood, Stephen Joseph and John Maltby detail how feeling grateful uniquely predicts life satisfaction.

Of note: Many are using the definition of happiness as "life satisfaction."

- From Texas A&M, psychologist and neuroscientist Joshua Hicks, and from Alto University in Finland, psychologist and philosopher Frank Martela, also reference the gratitude link: "We feel our existence is valuable when we take moments to appreciate beauty and cultivate a sense of awe."

Of note: You will frequently hear that feeling you are of value, and feeling validated, promotes happiness.

- The contagious effect. Cited by many, including James H. Fowler (professor of medical genetics and political science at the University of California, San Diego) and Nicholas Christakis (a physician and sociologist, Yale University), who found when a friend of yours becomes happy it increases your chance of happiness by 25%—and an additional happy friend increases the likelihood by 9%. I.e. just seeing someone else happy, can also make you happy!

- The Dalai Lama (2020) says organizing one's thoughts is key: "A disciplined mind leads to happiness, and an undisciplined mind leads to suffering."

- Socrates (circa 450 B.C.E.): "The secret of happiness, you see, is not found in seeking more, but in developing the capacity to enjoy less."

- A Swahili (African) proverb: "Patience attracts happiness; it brings near that which is far."

- A person's attitude! Happiness author Sonja Lyubomirsky emphasizes, "Your attitude and how you think and behave can have a lot of influence on your level of happiness."

- This author (right here! guiding you through this) prefers to emphasize a distinction between being happy in the moment (and perhaps a succession of such "hits") and being basically happy. "To be basically happy is the same thing as being psychologically healthy." As such, scrap a goal of "happiness" and strive instead to do what it takes to achieve mental health.

Time to release our Bird of Happiness? Not yet! Not yet! Here's my favorite, and allow me to introduce it, please, with "One man to find it all and in the light to bind them":

- Happiness psychologist Robert A. Emmons and his team at the University of California, Davis, evaluate all the happiness studies and integrate them with their own research. Dr. Emmons' overall assessment? Life satisfaction is "a belief in the interconnectedness of all life and a commitment to and responsibility for others."

SEPTEMBER 25

Does everyone have your hands in your lap? Rory?
Okay. We are going to learn a new song today! Actually, it's an old song, and maybe you already know it. Your mom or dad might have learned it when *they* were in preschool. A *looong* time ago—right?
We're sitting in a circle so we can all look across and see each other. Ready?

If you're happy and you know it clap your hands. (*clap clap clap*)
If you're happy and you know it clap your hands. (*clap clap clap*)
If you're happy and you know it, then your face will surely show it, if you're happy and you know it clap your hands. (*clap clap clap clap clap*)

If you're happy and you know it stomp your feet. (*stomp stomp stomp*)
If you're happy and you know it stomp your feet. (*stomp stomp stomp stomp stomp*)
If you're happy and you know it, then your face will surely show it, if you're happy and you know it stomp your feet. (*stomp stomp stomp stomp stomp stomp stomp*)
Clap your hands. (*clap clap clap clap clap clap clap clap clap*)

If you're happy and you know it shout "Hooray." (*Hooray!*)
If you're happy and you know it shout "Hooray." (*Hooray!*)
If you're happy and you know it, then your face will surely show it, if you're happy and you know it shout "Hooray." (*HOORAY!*)
Stomp your feet. (*STOMP STOMP STOMP STOMP STOMP...*)
Clap your hands. (*clap clap clap clap clap clap...*)

HOORAY!

SEPTEMBER 26

After a heady dose of research, analysis and statistics to gain insight into something dear to our lives, perhaps (do you suppose?) the same treatment could help us better understand the world's economic system. I'm struggling here, but the best poetic analogy I'm envisioning is a raven—(a sick raven?)—although I do love ravens!—and getting a grip on economics would be *so* beneficial to us all. It's just that the task is too overwhelming for me.
For those who do feel competent to provide both an overview and an analysis of economics— and for those simply trying to piece it together as best they can—I *can* offer the following observation as one of the smaller pieces of this perplexity to take into account:

When mom-and-pop businesses get bought out by large corporations, that which is special about them tends to go away. If the small business opens a local branch or two, I have seen that work, but even when it does their "specialness" takes a hit. Their specialness being the feeling that you are part of mom-and-pop's enterprise. That you know them personally—relishing their one-of-a-kind personalities!—and care that they prosper.—
With them knowing you, and caring that you (personally) get good service.
Feeling the bottom-level, gut-level, links of *family*.
Being directly involved with the actuality that "prosperity" means a lot more than financial success.

...And better yet, when the small business is part of a distinctive, unique community! By extension to feel personally invested—and valued—within your community's prosperity.

SEPTEMBER 27

Money... Money... Money...
That with which one purchases necessities, luxuries... a way of life. With coinage, banknotes, checks, automated transactions (where you never actually see or touch the money—creating a feeling that it's "not real"?). Sans money, the primitive bartering exchange—a trading of goods or services for goods or services. (Feels quite real!)

Money... Money... Money...
Feels great to have it. As if you're competent! Will be okay.
Feels wretched to not have it. *You are not competent.* (For shame.) Everything will *not* be okay.
There's something wrong (can you tell?) with both of those scenarios.

Another thought (yes, another piece to fit into the economy puzzle!):
The way most countries and societies are set up, an adult must possess money in order to obtain basic necessities. A major question being, how does one go about obtaining their money?
A detour here into male-female relationships. In Western European culture, sometime around the 18th century, women were becoming increasingly able to choose their own marriage partners and to marry for love. Doing so became romanticized—idealized—and those women who opted for money over love were scorned as materialistic and vane. As if they were thinking only of themselves.
Yet what is dearest to many women is the welfare of their children, or future children—that their their basic needs be met, and their health and life opportunities be optimized. What better way to secure their children's welfare than to prioritize wealth and status when selecting a mate?
Then as the middle class continued to swell, the immense gap between the dirt poor and the

aristocracy was being bridged, with many men's wages increasing. This enabled women to feel less pressure to marry "up" into wealth, as more men became suitable. It was especially good news for all the good men! who previously had been in the bottom echelon income-wise, who also prioritized the best for their children—and prioritized the women they cared about. Now they could afford to better care for them! (A tip of the hat to those men who so cared, and accordingly sacrificed for it.)

Although, excuse me for not *further* digressing into the Industrial Revolution, with its abysmal wages and working conditions for factory laborers, and the manner of the social upheavals—but the gist here being that throughout these changes, a middle class *was* emerging, with a more equitable distribution of monetary wealth.

Except... women were still feeling compelled *to get* married, as most were denied the means to earn a sustaining wage on their own—compounded with concern that their children be in competent hands while they were monetarily employed.

So... the good news! *At long last* (back to present century Western culture—which also includes many "minority" cultures, enriching and strengthening the whole)—*at long last!*—when a couple marries they can increasingly do it solely for love!—without the debilitating constraints the economic system has had them shackled to for generations.

Money... Money... Money...
And back to the initial question of how one goes about obtaining it. (*Whew!*)
To answer this, along with all the traditional ways, let's not overlook the option of a universal minimum income for all.

SEPTEMBER 28

There was a time—not long ago in the annals of human history—when the lives of "ordinary folk" followed a single path. They were born, had a childhood wherein they learned to be adults, followed by one shot at life. One good shot. If they messed up, they were lucky if they got another shot.

Preparation was essential to not messing up. For those fortunate enough to attend school, attending the "right" school made a difference. As did making the "right" contacts... marrying the "right" person... making "right" early job decisions...

All to set them on the best path.

Then, once on that path, came tenacity and making the most of it (whatever the path was). Securing a pension was often essential, so when their for-life job came to its end, they would have an income to sustain them through old age.

Note the job was "for life". Unless willing to say on the "bottom rungs" there wasn't much in the way of flexibility. To rise above the bottom meant more income and better benefits, which would be lost if you were to start over at the bottom of another job—which was where one was required to start!

To leave an unhappy marriage, for women, was encumbered with even worse life-plan options.

One life—one path—one good shot.

Modern life is much more forgiving! Divorces are easier to obtain, folks can switch jobs more readily and with more security, can retire for a few years then re-enter the job market—or can relocate and and embark on an entirely new career. All the while furthering your education either through classes or independently. The old-generation philosophy was that graduating from junior high or high school would be enough to have taught the youngsters of the community *all* they needed to know to get through life. Can you imagine your knowledge and your skills having ended there?

As harsh and unfair as the old systems were (with so many people stuck!) they nonetheless contained some underlying sensibilities worth salvaging. Having an abundance of safety nets in life and the ability to start over doesn't mean that first opportunities are to be taken lightly! Getting things right the first time can be deeply satisfying and can anchor one in to a full and ever-interesting life. Not all plants need repotting to thrive and grow (as one often hears these days). Sometimes with a little fertilizer, judicious pruning, and being turned into the light, a well-established plant will fill out optimally and produce its finest fruit. Never more true than with marriage! There will be difficulties to address and work through (always), but let's keep appreciating forever-marriages—and how they bind communities and families together. Those who manage to get marriage right the first time are to be congratulated.

Those who find a suitable career and fulfillment in developing it throughout their lifetime, are also a success story.

SEPTEMBER 29

Is your partner annoying you? (That does happen...) Is the *entire world* annoying you?
It is time to do—and a one and a two—

The mosquito swat! The mosquito swat!
Such a slight pest, everywhere, all about.
(Swatting the air! Swatting 'em out!)
Take that! Take that! Take that! Take that!

Then notice your partner, and help them swat theirs—
On their arms—on their legs—in the face—in their hair.
Then stop!—not to touch—stay your hand in the air.
You are now a statue.

A room full of statues—every-here. Every-where.
Your partners release you, maybe right. Or unfair,
With a slap to your hand. Putting it there!

The mosquito swat! The mosquito swat!
Everywhere, all about.
(Swatting the air! Swatting 'em out!)
Take that! Take that! Take that! Take that!

Swatting your partner—every which-where—
Stopping short! with your hand midair.

Partners release you by slapping that hand.
How long will it take? How long must you stand?

The mosquito swat! The mosquito swat!
Take that! Take that! Take that! Take that!

Swatting the air! Swatting 'em out!

—And now it's all over, and *IF* you had fun,
High-five with your partner! A dance well done!

[The music: An upbeat pleasant buzzing music. Not annoying.]

SEPTEMBER 30

A stoking of contentment into an off-guarded catch of realization. Chuckling.

OCTOBER

OCTOBER 1

Agreeably, your spouse is the best looking spouse on the planet.
(Agree?)
But if every spouse thinks so, how can this be?
Appear-ably, it can't be true.
(As in, way too many spouses!)
Yet *yours* is the handsomest, lovely-est, best-est looking!
Sincere-ably—endear-ably, so.
BECAUSE...
You wouldn't be in love otherwise.
Which is immutable. A truth.
Therefore it's a truth
That each foible—how interesting! Each blemish—*awwww*. Each distinction—*perfection!*
Endear-ably, sincere-ably—
So.

OCTOBER 2

Good morning! A surprise for you today—but remember, surprises come in all shapes and sizes, big ones and little ones. (So don't expect too much. I'm just announcing a *surprise*.)

So! Start by going about an ordinary day (*hum-drum—hum-drum—hum-drum...*) and provided nothing goes awry, you can pretty much guess how the day will go.
For a surprise, break from your usual thoughts and throw in a random flourish—by wondering about something you otherwise would take for granted.
For example, if driving a routine route into work—look!—a roadside sunflower. A beam of sunlight slashing across an old warehouse. Perhaps a fox streaking off into yonder shadows.
The "extra" wondering might be: That you could not have conjured that exact sunflower in your mind, it's specific location, its windblown profile—without having seen it. It was a surprise! The abandoned warehouse? The single moment of that one sunbeam romanticizing its rusticity was—that *one* moment. And... what other myriad moments of history—and secrets—might be associated with the derelict building? (Take your time pondering...)
The foxy-loxy! Where—*of all possible places?*—is it sprinting off to so intently? What are its concerns? *Who* is it??
As you continue on through your day, and the more unfettered you're allowing yourself to be, then the more observations and considerations you can slip on in.

...And it becomes not so much a matter of each day bringing new surprises to you, but you, by being who you are—bringing the new surprises of your thoughts and feelings to each day. For all of us.

OCTOBER 3

Singing yourself to new heights.
You can do this, because your soul can do this,
So your body can do this.
Climbing!
Up—UP!—
Singing yourself
Up!
Ascending...
Attending
To what is right. To becoming your best self.
Befriending
Your companions. Extending your help.
All upward. Everyone—*everything*—
UPWARD!
As notes rise, so your soul rises. Awaking!
Taking
You there. In the taking.

Chag Sameach!

OCTOBER 4

It won't be long before our neighborhood bears head on up into the Sandia Mountains for winter. This year we had a mama bear with her two first-season cubs pass through regularly!—and at least two lone males—one burly and fearsome, the other slightly built, perhaps an adolescent.

Our beleaguered apple trees have long since been stripped of fruit, with multiple broken branches, but we decided early on we'd rather offer nourishment to bears than wrap and secure the tree trunks. (One can always purchase apples from the market, whereas bears—they're special!)

No pesticides—meaning the bruins get a protein bonus of whatever crunchy and squirmy life is also availing themselves of the free snacks. Then, once sated, they will ofttimes loll around a bit under the trees, cubs playing, then lumber off toward the pond. Time for a dip!

This is where you come in—where I get to share this super-cool part with you!

Picture a lovingly landscaped lay of land anchored in serenity with a small, sparkling pond. A smattering of scrub oak branches arc over it, and surrounding it you see autumnal flowers and grasses, and—-*and!*—sprouting up from the pond—

Feet. *FEET!*

The plumply-padded soles of four *huge* black feet—as if growing there, like waterlilies do—with two hesitant cubs fidgeting on the bank.

(This scene goes away quickly, so hold onto it while it lasts!)

OCTOBER 5

The title for today's poem shall be—"Nuts Among the Leaves."
Or rather, let's call it—"Leaves Among the Nuts"—there being more nuts here than leaves.
    Rarely does one see so many acorns!
Or *maybe* (look at them scamper!)—"Squirrels Among the Acorns." That ought to hit the squirrel
    squarely on the head!—No!—Hit the nail squarely on the squeak—No! No!—let's hit
    the acorns squarely (crack!)—Yes—
And toss the meats out to this busy lot—
Who don't seem to need our help at all, actually.

Leaving us (*sigh*) with this hindsight title: "Save the Squirrels from All Manner of Nuts."

OCTOBER 6

To an erstwhile friend, a wish of peace.
I know things weren't going the way you had envisioned them, and hey (hands in the air) I back off.
What I hadn't known is that you were no longer a friend—and I'm wondering if you think you still are.
You used to be.
You seem to be expecting me to react as if *I* am still *your* friend.
I am not. Not your enemy either. I'm in a zone of neutrality regarding you.
Don't know *where* you are. You're acting all chaotic. Which is why the wish for peace.

It also means I won't be endangered from you, if you are at peace. (An ulterior motive.)
Nor will you be endangered from yourself.

You have so many talents and ambitions! Perhaps too many talents and ambitions. But know that there's a spot somewhere in life with your name written all over it. And with a few minor adjustments (always *some* adjustments)—the spot is a perfect fit. If you would only be open to seeing it!
If you would only stop trying so hard. Stop plotting and contriving and manipulating.
Stop being—greedy.
Your spot won't be society's most hailed, premier spot—but you already know that. You laugh about it. But it hurts. Your spot will be... well... *better* than that. Because your spot will hold *you*. And there's so much originality and goodness in you. (Being able to laugh at yourself, for one.)
My wish is that you realize...
Yourself.

OCTOBER 7

We float quiet and blithe as an abandoned cloud.
(*Quiet... Quiet...*)
A cloud on its own, as is. We float.
(*We float... We float...*)
A reassuring swoosh of flame.
(*Hishhh...*)

A majestic puffed-out canopy above us.
(*We float... We drift...*)

We are of the sky.
(*Quiet... Quiet...*)

We are of the sky... We are of the sky...

Vast panorama, far below.
A lazy, winding Rio Grande.
Bosque. Farms. Homes. Fields. Desert...
A vast panorama, muted. Still.
(*We float... We drift... Hishhh...*)

Quiet...

OCTOBER 8

The hawk doesn't like having to resort to our pond for water.
It must angle in carefully through a tangle of scrub oak and piñon branches to land at the water's edge.
Surely it would rather be winging high and afar!—landing on uppermost branches and mountain ledges, sipping from their caches of freshly pooled water.
But it's been a drought year. Wildlife is desperate. The drinking hawk radiates taut composure, launching up rashly at the slightest noise—
Thus bringing on its next problem: How to launch from within such an encumbered space? In a flurry of flurries it extends its awesomely wide wingspan, fanning the air trying to create enough lift—as it swiftly maneuvers out through the maze of branches. *Breathtaking!*
Utilizing every cubic foot of a confined cache of air. Escaping—on roiling breath of feather—
Through passages of last resort.

OCTOBER 9

Each clipped second of falling leaves
Offers a study of suspension.
A leaf may be caught mid-flip. It may be suspended mid-flutter. They may be slow motioned—
    clip clip clip—in a whorl of wind. A-flip. A-flutter. A-float.
Each on its way to its end.

Driving home from an outing through a lane of floating, flitting leaves,
Overhung by brilliantly dappled mother branches,
And undercrossed by crisp leaves swirling atop the pavement—
Is a drive through wistful endings.

OCTOBER 10

First snow floats softly
In kisses of fresh promise
And wonder bestilled.

OCTOBER 11

Away Outback
Is a way in to
A land of sun and kangaroo.
Where koalas snooze
And wombats squeal.
And blue heelers nip cattle heel.
Oww! Shove off.—
Heel!

Away Outback
It's fair-dinkum
To call *cooee* and let fate come.
Where wattles bloom, eucalyptus peel,
And blue heelers nip cattle heel.
Oww! Get lost.—
Heel!

Away Outback's
Wide ancient spaces
Vie with—*crikey!*—urban places.
Billabongs splutter. Lorikeets flutter.—
And blue heelers nip cattle heel.
Oww! Rack off!
Heel!

OCTOBER 12

It's dark in here, Mama.
Ka-bling-whoo thud.
Oh no, not again.
Ka-bling-whoo thud. Ka-bling-whoo thud.
Oh my, oh my.
Ka-bling-whoo thud. Ka-bling-whoo thud.
Are you all right, Jo-dunee?
Yes, I'm all right, Mama.
Ka-bling-whoo thud. Ka-bling-whoo thud. Ka-bling-whoo thud.
I wonder where we are now. Maybe I should look out.—
Oh no, can't look out. What might be out there?
My, oh my. What to do?
Must look out.—Just one little peek.
Oh my, oh *MY!* What was *THAT?*
Mama! Mama!
It's all right, Jo-dunee. It's only Jo-effina.
Oh, no. Oh, no... Jo-effina? Maybe just another little peek...
—OH NO! What was she doing?? She was peeking at—*ME!*
Maybe I should try again...
Let's see... Oh my! Yes! Oh my!
Is that what *I* look like? She's—um... um... lovely. Those perky things on top—ears?—they
       were so cute! Such intriguing—um... *eyes?*
I wonder what she thinks of me? Should I peek out again?
I wonder what all of life holds in store for me??
Ka-bling-whoo thud. Ka-bling-whoo thud.
Whoopsy. *Ahhh...* So nice and snug and safe in here.
So much to just ride out.

OCTOBER 13

A reoccurring question: *Are humans basically evil?*
An observation: Those who have not been allowed to mature sufficiently tend to think so, referencing—

Little ones who do not engage in playing, taking chances, making mistakes and learning from them—can form warped views about those who are doing all of these things.
Little ones who deny or indulge their angers without learning how to work through them, then when their angers burst forth randomly and inappropriately, are especially inclined to think this is the base nature of everyone. Evil.
Evil! That potent word again!
Yet, if these individuals care about others and want a world of peace and harmony, not rife with uncontrolled outbursts, then they are *not* evil. They care. They're good!
They have slipped into thinking everyone is fundamentally "evil" because that's how they interpret their own impulses—so they would attribute it to everyone else also.

Using themselves as a reference point, it would further follow that they would believe that if there was a universal basic income for all, then everyone would laze around unmotivated and self-indulgent. If that's what *they* would do.

OCTOBER 14

And a question even more avidly making the historical circuit:
What is the meaning of life?
And—*Wow!*—could there be a more poignantly confounding question?
It can be approached any which way—philosophically, metaphysically, theologically, psychologically, spiritually...
Perhaps which is why the question is so confounding—there being so many ways to consider it! To address it concisely, however, and in order to minimize overlappings that contradict each other, it can be broken down into two questions. One:
What is the meaning of your *life?* (For you, personally.)
This one being easy to answer (so let's get it out of the way because it's cluttering up the territory). The meaning of *your life* is—whatever *you* want it to be. (That's it!)
And likewise for each conscious being, the meaning of their life being whatever they want it to be, as each has their own values and concerns. So each establishes their own meaning for living.

The broader question, number two: *Why does life exist at all? Is there a masterplan, and if so, what is it, and to what end?*
Good luck if you want to take a stab at that one!
(Personally, I favor the simplicity of how E.O. Wilson, a sociobiologist, answered it.) (Before his last book, that is.)

OCTOBER 15

A dying moose's plea to the cougar:
Do you understand?

You have out-maneuvered me and outrun me. I have lost.
Do you understand what this means to me?

It was fair. I know you must do what you must do.
But please communicate you know the cost of your survival. Your awareness of my loss.

I am injured. There is pain. Please proceed quickly.

I am losing consciousness. But I know that what I am surrendering

Is a gift. It is my all and I don't want to give it unless
You understand—unless you know*—it is mine to give.*

OCTOBER 16

La luna llena bendecida. To be blessed by a full moon.
To glow. Within!
Wolves howl. Crime increases. Tides surge.
Something within you surges.
Physiologically, to be sure, but perhaps the moon is also pulling forth something more.
Within.
Could it be stillness that's surging? What a discomfort that would be for some! Something to defy.
For others, though, surging stillness could be their glow. As if enchanted.
A feeling to yield into. To know you're secure—tightly and warmly grounded—yet at the same time aware you're celestial.
The contradiction of that! The *truth* of that?
It doesn't make sense.
Yet—could that be the blessing the full moon casts down upon us? That when embraced within its glow, nothing is supposed to make sense. Just the glow itself.
Permeating.

OCTOBER 17

Ms. Linda! Ms. Linda! Rory's hurt!

Obviously! She's a shrieking, writhing bundle of pain, confusion—and outrage. But how badly hurt? She only sped her hot-wheels into a post. Nothing seems to be broken—some blood, though.

Hoisting her up onto the "nursing counter"—everyone gathered 'round, wide-eyed, shaken.—

Wounds gently and quickly patted clean with warm water, and soothing words. Amid the shrieks!... Amid the drowned-out, soothing words... The incessant screaming!... The quick calm tending... The mangled mess of tears, terror, tangled red curls, unrelenting pain.

She is locked into that first jolt when the crash occurred.

—All patched up now! Within a break of crying out, as she gasps in for yet another breath, I interject harshly, "You are not hurting anymore!" Before losing her momentary attention, I quickly elaborate, "Look down. It was a scrape on your knee. It's been cleansed, disinfected, and bandaged. *IT DOES NOT HURT ANYMORE.*"

Rory considers this. *Hmm—apparently true.* No longer trapped in that moment of Hell, she hops down and enthusiastically dashes off.

Imagine—as a fantastical conjecture—that you are lost in pain. Locked into it. You have died, and in that instant of dying—in a jolt of disbelief and panic—you are flooded with physical pain. It is all you feel. It goes on forever.

—Then STOP!—Think!—Remember these words. Let yourself break long enough to remember these words: "Look down, look down. *You have NO body.* THERE—IS—NO—MORE—BODILY PAIN."

OCTOBER 18

To swim with fishes is to swim with all the fishes that ever were.
To run wild with zebra is to run wild and engaged with the spirit of zebra. With all the zebra who
    ever were.
To swing with monkeys, to fly with insects, to socialize with humans—the part of you that is
    open to them becomes one with them.
A universal aligning of minds which is said to form a
Singularity.
A whole of acceptance that fits "right" with all.
Or which breaks down into specifics—at the will of the being.
In spirit.

OCTOBER 19

Lightning flashes!
Deep resonating *BOOOM—BOOMS!*
As if the sky above is cracking open.
As if the reliable continuity of the heavens is breaking apart.
Sudden, jagged openings into—
Brightness as intense as the sun!
Sudden, jagged openings into—
The unknown? *BOOOM—BOOM!*

Deep, preternatural resonating.
—*Ka-BOOM!* Flash!—
Alarm! Alarm of—the unknown? Feeling trapped—within the resonating?
—*Ka-BOOOOM!* Flash!-Flash! BOOM!—rumble—*BOOM!*—
Oh, to be held tight by another person. Tight! To quell the *BOOM*s and flashes.
The unstoppable cracking-open flashes—revealing what?
Charged flashes revealing—*triggering?*—bright insights?
Insights into—the unknown?
Insight into how brave you are, or are not? That you can, or cannot, handle this? Flash!—
     BOOM!—
Alarm!
Flashes of insight into—
Devastation.

...The thrill!

OCTOBER 20

As a maxim: *Treat others as you would have others treat you.*
Now that's one to think twice about.
For example, imagine a father who always wished *his* father had directed him into sports—so he relentlessly pushes his own son into sports. He'd be doing what he wished had been done to him. *But—*
What if that man's son is non-athletic and feels incompetent when competing physically?
Or a mother who wishes *her* mother had bugged off and let her do whatever she wanted—so she "kindly" lets her daughters run amok...
A dietician whose body craves legumes, so guess what her clients are advised to consume in large quantity...
A drug addict who "generously" shares his stash with his non-addicted friends...
Not to mention—lest we forget!—masochists. Those who derive pleasure from having others inflict pain and degradation upon them. Would you want such a person going around treating you—treating *everyone*—that way?
Thinking twice! before spreading advice.

OCTOBER 21

An anguish: So much for the advice of being brave and facing one's problems! There are times when doing *that* can sure make things worse! Like—say—this morning?
Not that there aren't times when it's best to face problems and solve them, but what about, say—*this morning?*
Face the truth whatever it may be. (*Yeah, right.*) What about when the truth, and the issues, and the facts are such a huge, tight, entangled knot that they *cannot* be untangled? Impossible.
Did the advice givers ever consider *THAT* possibility?
How to know when to face problems—and when to let them be?

OCTOBER 22

Peeking out from under the covers. Perhaps this is one of those days when it's best to not get out of bed.
Hasn't anyone else looked outside lately? Big, bad world out there!
Nice, safe bed in here.
Something coming down today that you know—*you know*—you're not up to dealing with. Beyond your capability...
But it *has to be* dealt with.
...Or does it? Maybe by staying unavailable here this morning—buying time—then the worst of it will simply blow over? But it *won't* simply blow over. It *must* be dealt with. And *you* MUST get up and get out there and do this!
And it will be your fault when you fail. You know this.
Is it possible to feel more—alone?
Doesn't anyone else know, *really know*, what dread is?

OCTOBER 23

Peeking out from under the covers. Well, you did it. The worst is over—which is the good news. You did however—indeed—alas—as you knew would happen—fail. *But it's over with!*
Life goes on. Sometimes other people, in other situations, are not so fortunate, to be able to keep going on after their incompetencies.
And the damage wasn't as bad as it could have been. Damage and fallout, there was—indeed—and pieces to be picked up. But at least there are pieces to be picked up!—And a few shining ones among them. And there will be opportunities to assemble life better in the future. But—
Still peeking out...
Dare you allow yourself to feel it? Yes? Yes! There is... Hope! The belief that life can be good —maybe *even better* next time around. *But...*
About that hope—maybe some caution? Can one go overboard allowing hope? Yesterday there was no hope—*none at all*—an impossibility of success. Yet the impossibility concerned only that one situation. Now life affords new situations, and there are reasons to be hopeful!
...Right? ...*Right??*
Hopeful as regards the new possibilities—one can be hopeful *about them*. (Got that part right!) But what about *overall* hope? That life is basically good and worth living. Did you impinge upon that?
And how much of the fallout that's ruinous is yours to address?
Should you get up and get on with it, believing that *everything* will be all right now?

OCTOBER 24

Is it the flutter, or the flitter?
Or perchance a quaking?
Listen—was that not a twitter?
Buoyancy a-waking.

Is this now song, or sorrow drifting?
Caught in with love together.
Be it joy? Or hearts a-shifting—
All hearts! Of a feather.

OCTOBER 25

What can be said about someone who herself had the perfect words to say about everyone?
One can only fall short.
Not just short of the perfect words, but short of the equanimity underlying them.
The sense of humor—warm humor—that stirs her readers to feel all is basically right with the world.
Even her scoundrels can be understood, accepted—
And in a manner wherein justice prevails.
Jane Austen.
Yet in Ms. Austen's lifetime, despite her splendid contributions, she herself was not as splendidly appreciated.
Her novels make one feel that life is worth living—yet she died young. With pain.
Wish we could all collectively just give her a big hug.

OCTOBER 26

There is a type of forgiveness that happens before one has even been wronged.
An attitude that evil does exist—unmitigated, cruel evil—and that there will be times you are
    trespassed against—
But not to take the trespassing personally.
Even when it is meant to be personal.
An attitude of not bothering to hate.

OCTOBER 27

Turns out there's a trick for pulling oneself up by the bootstraps.
You surmise—*a magic trick?* Right? Because it defies the laws of physics for one to pull themselves up by their own bootstraps!
It does indeed. Nevertheless, the proffered idea for today calls attention to this legit trick.
Because—
Sometimes those who have been knocked down by life can... *hocus-pocus!*... pull themself up without relying on fair and righteous laws.
Which is the gist of it! Not relying on anyone or anything but oneself. Heave-ho, up you go!
...Except it's not easy, and it's not fair either, which is the gravity of it. You're the victim here, so why should *you* be the one having to go through the hardship of exerting yourself *on top of everything else?*
It's not fair!
But where will you be if you don't? Lying there on the ground, garnering sympathy—and (would you dare?)—blame any who are trying to help for not succeeding in getting you up?
They can't do it! They're your friends, they're trying. Appreciate them! *Only you* can do it.—
And you do it by caring about others more than yourself. Even if it's just caring about one small pet (a cat?)—that alone can be enough to get you back up on your feet. You do it so you can help someone else.—
And as a by-product of that—look!—you're back on your feet!

OCTOBER 28

Oh, to be an owl!
    Oh, really?
Yes! No need for sarcasm. Owls are awesome.
    I agree.
(Humph.) To start over:
Oh, to be an owl! To soar the prescient shades of night,
Sweeping swift on tilted wing, banking sharp!—
To plummet...
    Cut! Cut!...
What now?
    Not sure you understand owls. What's to exalt about being a predator?
To continue! To plummet bold where movement quickens...
    You mean where MICE quicken...
Yes! Where harmless cute little mice quicken!...
    Rooting for the mouse here...
Where stark intent and gambits thicken!
Twists of fate, all-ness-es given.
Oh, to be—
[in unison] The owl.

OCTOBER 29

Bats cut the sky with little snips.
The black sheet of a night sky—
Cutting it with little jagged snips that
Quicken into more jagged snips—and *more* jagged snips!—
Quick! Quick! Quick! *Snip! Snip! Snip! Snip!*—
Until the black sky is ripped open
Into a plethora of even blacker wings, chaos, and intrications.

OCTOBER 30

Tell me once again why we're doing this. We are sensible adults. Why should we enter this forest dark and drear? WHAT? Well, okay—but if we don't make it out alive, this is all your fault.

Trepidly, trepidly, on we go, deeper, deeper into the gloom. Following a narrow, hidden path—but whose path is it? Did foraging deer trample it down, roving from one promising clearing to another? Not much feels promising in here, though. And if not a deer path—then whose?
We are trespassing. The feeling is certain. But upon whose territory do we infringe?
Be there hostile, lurking enemies about?
Or—is it possible we are our own worst enemies? Never knowing when we'll trip over a twisted root... stumble off into a ravine... slip into an unforgiving bog...
Has it become too dark to see? Shadows keep deepening. Merging. Closing in...
Has it become too quiet to hear? Too much silence. Closing in...
Have there become too many unknowns to—reason?
Does not dark magic coalesce in voids of reason?
Closing in... Closing in...

(*Crunch.*)
AAAAAAH!

OCTOBER 31

Tired of being your same-ol' self?
Do you find yourself constricted? Conflicted?—
ESCAPE! (Tee-hee—yes!—*giggle*.)
Superheroes! Alter-egos! Devil-may-cares—caring that they aren't to care. *YES!*
Traipse and slither...
Dance and dither!
Now's your night to play it out. Fresh perspectives *flung!* about.
(Tee-hee—ha-ha—harumph-harumph—*chortle*—*cackle*...)

NOVEMBER

NOVEMBER 1

In a murkiness of time. In the cirque-ness one finds…
We are here.
The dead.
Our bodies were formed by the time we drew our first breath, which was when our sensations and intellect entered fully into your empirical world.
We lived our lives until our bodies wore out or were otherwise terminated. The physical falling away, but the physical had only helped create who we have become.
We are here.
Every thought we had, every interaction, made us real in other dimensions simultaneously with our growing selves in the dimensions known to you. We existed in that larger reality that remains ever. As we remain ever, now free from earthly constraints. But also sometimes missing the physical life we had.
Perhaps missing you in particular. Whenever we like we can be aware of you. Each of us can use our energy to stimulate new thoughts in our minds, and in so doing create new bonds, or reinforce old ones. Perhaps bonds of love. If you and I love each other, our love can be never-ending. If we focus and make it never-ending.
We can visit together and connect not only on these days you celebrate Dia de los Muertos, but whenever we each open up our minds and reach out to one another.

NOVEMBER 2

Once upon a time…
Were you looking forward to solving your own problems, achieving your goals, and entering into a bright future?
Secure that the good things in life would always be there—*especially* solid foundations—confident *they* don't go away. Solid foundations are *solid,* to be built upon! And the good things you enjoy—they were to be expanded and incorporated into the bright future.
Did that *feel right?*—in the unaccountable way perceptions can make sense.
So many young folk are grounded in such confidence and sense—and forge ahead!

Until one day, it comes to pass…
One reaches for a favorite mug to enjoy hot cocoa—and it's not there. Lost in transit, or broken somewhere along the way.
Something taken for granted. No more to be.
A dear friend who has gone their separate way, now each of you too busy and preoccupied to share time together.
A dear friend—dead.
A stroll along a lovely blossoming avenue in your hometown—but the trees have long-since been bulldozed down, clearing way for—asphalt.
Your hometown—home state—your country? You never meant to leave it *forever*. Somewhere in the back of your mind imagining it would always be there for you—when the time was right—because that is where, somehow, you belong. When did you make the decisions, one little innocuous decision upon another, that eliminated that possibility?

But can not the good things and the good times, as memories, always remain a part of us?
Perhaps you ask, what would be the point, if the sensory and emotional input is no longer happening. If that was what you valued. That which is gone.
And when you let go of it—when and if you ever mentally let go of it—then it really will be

…The end.

NOVEMBER 3

Imagine a night so dark—so unequivocally dark—that there is nothing but blackness. Absolute *blackness.*

Then a minuscule break in the blackness—*twink!*—then gone. Too small to have registered, smaller than a pinprick, but it WAS. And its mere existence puts lie to the totality of darkness.

Then another spark of light!—*twink*—gone! And another—*another!*—enough fleeting sparks to have now become visible. You know they're there! Little sparks of—

Hope?

Hope in a world with so much darkness?

But hope for what? And whose hope? These tiny feeble twinkles.

Which are now gone.

—*They're back!*

Just a smattering. Twinkling. *Hope!*—Hope for goodness. For everything good, and right, and for all to be well. For all life's heartening possibilities.—

Proliferating into—an inundation of possibilities! *Everywhere*—flickerings and sparklings. Candles! Clay lamps! Against the omnipresent backdrop of—absolute black.

Is the surge of flickering in contrast to the blackness, or integral to it? As one exists, so must the other? To acknowledge this whole, in... Hope.

A celebration that good can triumph over evil, knowledge over ignorance—the sparking of life! over desolation.

This Festival of—*LIGHTS!*

NOVEMBER 4

Is there color within color?
Light within light?
Definitive shades of being, each the one-and-only, of permanent combinations?
Blends of only one same tone.
Ommmm...

Is there a single way to view all which is changing?
A multi-dimensional confluence.
Ommmm...

Each dimension transparently apparent.
Each shade and tone distinct.
Distinctly—the same.

Everything suffused within everything else.
Chaos suffused within order.

To contemplate everything and nothing. Simultaneously.
As the same thing.

Ommmm...

NOVEMBER 5

My! Oh my! The octopi
Occupy their place in the ocean by mimicking
The ocean.
Undulating smoothly across sandy stretches, or
Shape-shifting into a tight bumpy blob, as if they are a rock.
By changing color—as the ocean swiftly changes color—or in fluctuating their patterns of color,
In the manner of fluctuating shadows.
By changing *texture*—mantles becoming spiky like algae.—
But mostly by flowing, rolling over rocks and boulders into crevices.—
To the point where one can ask oneself, is there an intelligent life form here, with a soul? Or just
      more ocean—flowing and churning, obliterating the possible mysteries within?

My! Oh my, the octopi occupy not only a place in the ocean,
But a place in our restive yearning to fill in the blanks of everything awesome, and to pin down
      —comprehend—what awesomeness is.
How important is "awe" in our lives?

NOVEMBER 6

Being—*In Love!* (Spring blossoms drifting down, blessing all upon whom they alight.)
Several ways to have gotten In Love. One way is to have fallen—perhaps hard. (Bam! Splat?)
Or to arrive In Love rationally, carefully, opening yourself up to it bit-by-bit.
Those who walk around in a state of complete openness are at highest risk of tripping up and becoming the ones who *fall* into it.

Being—In Love! (Leaves burgeoning, unfurling, reaching out into sunshine.)
But does it make sense? Being In Love.
Couldn't it be considered irrational to put the welfare of another above your own? (As in, what kind of survival trait is that?) But there you find yourself doing it! And it *does* make sense from a deeper-than-rational point of view. (Does *that* make sense?) Shall we call in a socio-biologist? Discombobulating—and delightful!—to try to reconcile the contradictions.

Living with being—In Love. (Storms shake and batter the branches, stripping them of bark and leaves.)
You might decide this isn't worth it, or you might simply realize you've fallen *out* of Love. (Either of these cases being more likely to happen if lust or neediness were paramount when you initially became In Love. Take away the lust or need—and what's left?)
Determination, heartfelt vows and stubbornness won't be enough to bring back something that didn't set in and take root.

Another possibility: You had not been In Love—but hadn't know you weren't. Just thought you were.

And *another* consideration: There are ways of intimately cohabiting with someone, without "being In Love" as part of the equation. Maybe it's for convenience, with a mutual respect and love (but not "being In Love")—if that's what works best for you both.

Other cohabitation possibilities you've probably noticed include a business-type arrangement, or, with each partner "mutually using" the other, in a game, with each "cleverly" trying to gain the most advantage. When partners are up-front that it's a game, and are equally matched so it's more-or-less balanced—no problem? (And maybe fun?)

True, forever being—*In Love?* YES! (A rugged beautiful tree, now deeply rooted, having survived many seasons.)

Having begun with trust and wonder, but then—*surprise!*—when rather than just settling in, the wonder took root and *kept growing*. To not have expected it. Yet perhaps not counting on it happening had something to do with why it was able to happen? (Something about not counting one's chickens before they're hatched?)

Yet there your tree stands! Trust having paid off. Gratitude galore. *AND*—*yet another* opportunity to notice that love is *expansive*. Everything that helps your beloved flourish also becomes beloved... Then everything that helps those things flourish become part of the love also... Then, adding in all that helps *them* flourish...

Vulnerability falls aside. There is strength here.

NOVEMBER 7

We all feel bonds and connections with the world around us. There are bonds of love. There are bonds of duty, which can be imposed upon us externally by law or convention—or bonds that we feel on a gut-level must be honored. Or we might simply be *predisposed* to feel bound to someone or something—
But know we're free to override the feeling and do whatever we want.
In order to make the best decisions regarding whether and when to override bonds, it helps to sort through them and know where you stand. A lot to break down here! Starting with—

Bonds imposed upon us. Laws of the land, rules of society or rules of your household. Religious mandates. You take risks if you don't abide by these rules!—or at least give the impression you are abiding by them. Can you list what laws and regulations are being forced on you? To what extent do you feel "bound" by them? If not totally on board, be careful when making—

Commitments. If you don't like the rules you're living under, you might want to remove yourself to a different situation. Or attempt to change the rules. In the meantime, making as few commitments to them as possible, because commitment bonds can be hard to honorably extricate oneself from.

Emotional bonds. In particular, bonds of love. (Take a breath! Ready?) These are bonds coming from within—from within our bodies, and indeed—yes—involving *our souls*. (On to that next.) For now, as regards our physical bodies, multiple processes are at play "telling" us to make certain decisions, and it feels right when we do. From conception our developing endocrine system, and the hormones it regulates, start having a say in our composition. Hormones are integral with *how we are formed!*—and it feels comfortable going along with them.

Neurological processes are even more spectacular. (Anything involving sparking is spectacular!) Neurons are nerve cells, and there are neurotransmitters within our bodies (set in play from conception, remember) that begin actively transmitting "information" from neuron to neuron. (Either electrically or chemically.) Thought patterns are being established. A mature human brain is complex and has approximately 100 billion neurons. (A mature elephant brain is also complex and has approximately 250 billion neurons.)

All this physiology making our bodies what they are! You are probably familiar with "genetic codes"—a set of instructions in our genes encoded in DNA double-helices, passed from parent to child. There is also speculation, currently being researched, that there is a type of "cellular memory" within a body's cells that stores memories of brain processes, and when these cells are removed and implanted within another person, then some "memories" of the donor person are transferred as well.

Is your mind boggled yet? (All your billions of neurons, and the synapses busily firing off between them!) *But hold onto your hat as we get to this part—*

Psychic links.

Yes. Psychic bonds among all beings who possess minds. One can ignore them or block them out (and may be well advised to do so)—but *something exists* that they would be blocking out.

For example, twins who feel mentally linked, but not of our known physical world. Those who sometimes know what the other is thinking and feeling. Even when spatially separated. There are even accounts of twins knowing what the other is thinking and experiencing when they have been separated at birth and *don't even know they have a twin.* Just "unaccountable" images and feelings will occur to them. (And which are easily dismissed as dreams.)

This phenomenon has also occurred with mothers who have given their babies up for adoption, at birth, where both mother and child experience flashes throughout their lives of where the other is and what they're engaged in.

Modern science has yet to explain these occurrences.

And when the occurrences do happen, the individuals involved have made decisions and adjusted their lives in accordance with the other person, because it emotionally felt comfortable—and "right."

Shared patterns of thought—images—personal tastes and preferences—not only set in motion prenatally, but of course happening after birth as well. So many possibilities! Siblings who emotionally and mentally bond... The bonding of unrelated children who shared childhood experiences... Parents whenever they are "open" to their child's heart and mind...

Note the word "open." A certain kind of openness? Is that when these psychic bonds form? Falling in love! Feeling an unguarded gratitude toward someone... While liking and connecting with someone's ideas... While experiencing the "rightness" of a core of a religion...

In particular—feeling a bond with any and all who understand you... who have shared any fraught experience with you... with those who have seen you at your best...

It sure would help to know, when making important life decisions, the assorted physical, emotional and mental predispositions going into those decisions. Enabling you to wield control of when you decide to yield into them and when not.

When opening up to psychic realms in dimensions unknown to us, because they are unknown, it pays to tread especially carefully. Psychics do. Because of the dangers. If one were to open up indiscriminately to any and all bodiless persons, imagine all the angry and cruel restless spirits who might descend upon them. *Into* them. This is the stuff of nightmares, horrors. One must learn how to focus on which persons *they* want to connect with!
If left to the spirits doing the selecting, there is some evidence that they are drawn to living persons with similar thought patterns. Someone they were bonded with in life, perhaps, or if the living person is in a problematic situation, or hurting, in a manner similar to what they had lived through. The bodiless person might care and want to help since they now know what is needed.

If you "felt" a sympathetic presence wanting to help you, would you take a chance on letting them "in"? It could bolster your confidence and energy. Or—

If you are vengeful, violent and hateful, that might be the kind of spirits you're attracting (having similar mental processes) and they would enjoy making you feel worse. Even if you're not hateful and violent, simply vulnerable and insecure, cruel spirits would enjoy tormenting you.

The bottom line regarding connecting with the minds of others, both living and dead? Just stay tight with whomever is worthy of your love—figure out who those people and animals are—and stay tight with *them*.

NOVEMBER 8

I love it when…
Squirrels dash across an open space.
Bushy-long-tailed squirrels. Lengthy open space. Must quickly get to the other side!
A fluidity of energetic leaps. Pointy nose first. Long stride with lowered rump—elevated rump!
    —down rump—*quick!* high rump—low rump—*fast-fast!*… Tail flowing behind each
    bound, mistily fluffy—
All blending together into one long fluid flow.
Into one long perfection.
Something to get lost in!

Okay!—Your turn.
You love it when…

NOVEMBER 9

I *super* love it when...
I walk into a room filled with books!
Shelves upon shelves—stacks upon stacks—a myriad of intrigues!—spilling over onto armchairs, side tables, footstools...
Slight musty smell. Quiet. The reverent quietness of many minds having been here before.
Feeling safe.
Safe within the myriad of ideas and adventures and knowledge and very lives of people. The fullness of humanity!—
And that those in this room went to the trouble of writing themselves down, and that someone exerted themself to acquire and accumulate them here, some of the volumes bound handsomely and lovingly, and I feel as if it was all done—*for me?* It feels like it. It feels —personal. And tangible.
I feel welcome and understood in a room full of well-worn, musty old books.

Back to you!
You feel welcome and understood when...

NOVEMBER 10

Singular among poets, Emily Dickinson knew how to take a human perception, crystalize it into an understanding, then crystalize the understanding into words. Bright, tight gems of words. An artistry she delighted in.

Regarding Emily's personal life, she didn't have many options, but between tedious domestic duties she was able to sneak in time to sequester herself and write, write, write—exquisitely arranging her heart.

Yet throughout this she kept trying to create more options for herself. To *embrace* more options.

Emily kept reaching out to the world via letters—ofttimes effusive letters—brimming with honesty and hope. It was a type of fishing. But her letters netted nothing much worth keeping. Her recipients likely felt imposed upon, rather than flattered by the opportunity to become part of her life. (And which would have been mortifying to her, to the extent she picked up on this.)

Biographers tend to leave Dickinson's life with the facts, what actually happened (very little) and why, but perhaps speculation of "what might have been" could bring us closer to understanding this bravely open, honest—and overlooked—person.

What if Emily had been able to engage more fully with the world?

What if she had snagged, made commitments, and followed through with what she was fishing for?

Or—*what if* she had felt it necessary to become monetarily employed? Or felt it her duty to marry a particular person? To have children?

Within any of these alternative lives, would she have still written her poetry? If so, would the poems have been the same?

Was Emily Dickinson's life a series of disappointments, struggles and defeat? Both she and her poetry having gone unrecognized in her lifetime.

Was she lonely?

Or by mastering her artistry—by not compromising her style, her sincerity, or her sense of self—had Emily on the deepest level mastered her life? She remained ever-thoughtful, ever-bright, ever-playful.

Was she able to feel successful?

NOVEMBER 11

Another Emily poet. Ms. Emily Bronte. Hard hitting poetry. *Wham!*—to the point. As Em herself says, "No coward soul is mine."

No indeed—one cannot accuse her of that! What one might accuse her of, were her poetry to be compared to Shakespeare's, is that her precision is intermittent. She tends to go out on limbs making assumptions, but once you see what her assumptions are—especially the times you agree with them—then her precision is stark and stunning.

Although it is perhaps not fair to compare her poetry to Shakespeare's because, for one, Bronte's scope incorporates not just human nature, but *all* of nature, whereas Shakespeare more-or-less limited himself to human situations, motivations and feelings. Easier to be precise when working within narrower parameters.

It can further be said that Bronte and Shakespeare were masters of the craft of poetry, as opposed to being masters of the *art* of poetry (which plays around with evocations).

Emily Bronte's personal life? Ahh. Here is where *biographers* go out on limbs making assumptions. It is fairly clear that among her family's four surviving siblings (all spaced only about a year apart) that Emily ended up in the role of the "tough guy." This freed her younger sister Anne from having to do it, who otherwise might have, but whether this "gift" to Anne was intentional is unknown. (I like to think Emily was at least aware of it, and that it entered into her decision.)

"Big sister Charlotte" kept trying to be in charge of them all, but apparently didn't understand what was going on and kept attributing selfish, bossy motives to Emily (and to their overwhelmed brother). Interesting that what Charlotte accused them of is what she herself was.

A tight mess of bold, intense, independently-minded siblings!

Yet if they had been in a different life situation—imagine each a single child and raised with a non-provocative parent—it would have been a different story. In that case it would have been, for me, a special joy to have known Emily and to have watched her blossom.

As it was, she kept pushing the envelope—her own personal envelope and all of life's boundaries—wringing out as much drama from them as she could. Didn't know when to stop, to ease up on herself.

Yet if she had eased up, could she have been effective in her role of the family's tough guy? Didn't Emily need that edge and lack of grace in order to get things done that needed to be done? In order to be the good person she was.

Consider it a trap. And Emily Bronte, like so many others who would have preferred a different role in life, was apparently caught up in it.

P.S. to Emily:

I hope you know your description of the Yorkshire moors is exhilarating and unrivaled! And I stand both agape and delighted that you dared refer to God as your slave. "*My slave, my comrade, and my king.*" (A "slave" because if God is Nature, then Emily, being part of Nature, in some ways controls it.) While aware your father is a fiery, opinionated preacher! (I'm crumpling up laughing here...)

NOVEMBER 12

In a "perfect world" would abundant, trap-free opportunities be available to all people?
    Opportunities for each individual to be optimally educated and to fully develop their unique talents? If this were to come about, would the whole of society be improved?

Such a societal state has been dubbed a "meritocracy"—a concept which warrants examining.
    The present concept of meritocracy is that it's where each person gets to "rise" according to merit.

But rise in what, and is there room in "the top" for all qualified and deserving individuals?

Would maximizing opportunities for everyone equate with maximizing their happiness and fulfillment?

One unsettling thing meritocracies do is take away the excuses of those who do not "succeed." In the past those "on the bottom" could always claim unfairness. Perhaps revel in unfairness—how if only they'd had the chance they'd be rich and famous. Saving face.

Also, in a meritocracy as presently envisioned, where would those fit in who are disinclined to embrace the offered opportunities?

Would those living quiet, virtuous lives be considered just as important as those living louder, more famous lives?

And what about the randomness—and sheer luck!—of those who snag "top" positions?—beginning with the *impossibility* of all equally qualified children to be accepted into "the best" schools. Would graduates of such schools be inclined to consider themselves "better" than those who had been equally qualified but not admitted?

Perhaps worse—would those unable to graduate from "top" schools, plus those who did not (randomly!) obtain the most coveted positions in society, be inclined to consider themselves "lesser" than those who did?

Then envision the ideal—the justice if the glut of life-traps was reduced! If equitable educational opportunities were available to all! If there were better and more abundant opportunities for career and life enrichment!

How could this come about?

And who is it who's defining "merit," anyway?

Perhaps it is time for each of us (wherever we stand in society's hierarchy) to define for ourselves what merit is—and the best way to honor it.

With a vital observation for those on the so-called bottom rungs:

Please know the majority of those in society's so-called top rungs do not look down on you as a lesser human being. *The majority.* The *minority* who do may get more publicity, but most college grads and white-collar professionals are working hard to do their part in making our country a better country and our world a better world. They do this in friendship—including *to you*—and may well think whatever you're doing with your life is cool.

NOVEMBER 13

An epiphany!
For the old man—now bursting with news!—to have at long last solved the mystery—for all humankind!—of what life is for!
And to think it took nearly dying to see it.
But he *didn't die!* It was when the pall of death lifted and he knew he was going to pull through —that was when it was all so obvious—
Right in front of him! His blanket. To pull it up snug under his chin and feel warm. Cosseted.
Soft wooly slippers. A mug of chicken soup. *Oh yes!* This is what makes life worthwhile!
Every other aspect of living (this is the obvious part!) serves only to augment this experience. His life's work—those he loves—his hobbies and passions and everything else he holds dear—the greater they are, then the greater the experience of being snug and alive under a warm blanket.
But if he were to attempt sharing this astonishing insight, wouldn't he be considered—senile? Delirious? ...*A simpleton??*
And—*oh!*—a book, too. Someone reading him a book. His mother's voice sing-songing nursery rhymes. (*Giggle, giggle.*) *That silly goose!*

NOVEMBER 14

Ding! Ding! Ding! Warning! Warning!
If there is someone you are responsible for—such as an elderly person, a child, or perhaps a delightful dog—and you love that person, then
Be alert to not cut corners on their care.—
Simple and inexpensive things that are easy to let slide, such as routine dental care or opportunities for exercising.
Because!—(among other negatives)—
Then you will be inclined to not exercise or take adequate care of your own health.
So then there would be *two* of you. Untended. (*Twice* as not good.)
Because once you accept that a treatment is okay for someone you love, then there's guilt if you were to "indulge" in it yourself.

NOVEMBER 15

When is a mistake not a mistake?
(*What?*)
Go away. A mistake is not a mistake when you are so slow on the uptake
     That you never catch on to what's at stake.
     No regrets.
And *THEN* what you did is not a mistake.
It is... You.
Who you have become.

NOVEMBER 16

Sun rays break through the lifting mid-morning fog,
Immersively brightening the day below as smoothy and swiftly as melting whipped cream.
As wide and glowing as a translucence of swelling music.
A certainty of renewed hope!
Then just as swiftly, smoothly and widely—
Rescinds the dream.

NOVEMBER 17

You are probably already well-versed in the answer to today's question: "What are prayers?"
At least you have probably formed a *working answer*. Here's toward pinning down the practice with more exactitude:

Are prayers focused well-wishes for another person or for a desired event to happen? Everyone has such desires at times! Are we "sending off" prayers when we do?
Must such desires be formally ritualized in accordance with a particular religion? (Specifically addressed to a god, for example.)
Must they be formatted into words? For example, would simply intensely wishing for something to happen constitute a prayer?

Do prayers work? That is, do they help bring about the desired result?

What if you were to pray for someone who doesn't want to be prayed for? Would it be disrespectful to pray for them anyway?
They might have a good reason for spurning your interference—a none-of-your-business reason. Could praying for them anyway make their lot in life worse?

Does the sincerity level or intensity level of prayers make a difference? For example, would a half-hearted or forced prayer be less likely to be effective?

If one fervently wishes someone ill (as in a curse), might that "work" also?

Let's say prayers are only to bring about positive events. That they stimulate and facilitate caring.

And that by using one's mind to visualize something good and healthy—and focusing on the vision—and by being open-minded about how it may come about—
That our world really does become a better place, because of prayers.

How powerful such thoughts might be!

NOVEMBER 18

A ferret is... A smile! A perky, furry face, alive with questions, unable to keep its long flexy body
      from squirming, wriggling, twisting, contorting
In my granddaughter's arms.
No... No... There's more going on here.
A smile is the *second* ferret,
Wriggling over and around the first ferret and into and through my granddaughter's blouse.
No...No... That's not it either. Could it be the *third ferret* that makes the smile? Astro!
      Incessantly wrapping himself tight and snuggly around the squirming others.
A felicity of ferrets, to be sure! Quite a smile!—But we're still missing something here...
Got it!
A smile—*the true smile*—is the smile on my granddaughter's face.

NOVEMBER 19

Greetings fair goose, fat goose.
I will hold you.
I am around you and above you.
Golden sunlight will pass through me and strike upon your feathers.
Fine white feathers, beating slowly, rhythmically, parting my silken thickness and sending small swirling currents into me.
They tickle me.
You will fly into nighttime where silver moonlight catches transparently in my breath, and will illuminate your course.
I love experiencing your sleek body slipping smoothly through the glow.
There will be rain. It is heavier than I and will punctuate your journey with hundreds of tiny drops, reminding us of both burdens and frivolities.
The clouds will part. Vistas and destiny are ours!
We embrace them together.
Fair goose, fat goose, you will grow thinner, wearier. You will leave me.
You are my rhapsody.
I will kiss you goodbye.

NOVEMBER 20

Imagine having the freedom to determine your own path in life!
Regardless of what life you born into or how you were raised, to have been given the gift of education and of opportunities.
Perhaps not the best of educations or a completeness of opportunities,
But to know your predecessors cared and did what they could—and that many still care and are still contributing what they can.
Those who came before didn't have to. They could have forced you into their own little boxes, to enhance and justify their own lives. The gift of freedom, and in a manner that stimulates the freedom of others, is no trifling legacy.

With thanks to all who have provided and who keep perpetuating this legacy.

NOVEMBER 21

To be grateful is to relax into a consciousness of life's delights.
To relax into a consciousness of life's delights is to be grateful.

NOVEMBER 22

The talking heads—*blah-blah-blah*. Telling you what to think—*blah-blah-blah*. Then demanding, *Do you understand?*—DO YOU UNDERSTAND?
Well, that's a yes, you understand.
You understand they're an idiot.
Putting you in the unfortunate and intense position of having to decide whether, or what, to reply.

NOVEMBER 23

To a certain person: I don't do it for you.
The occasional dinners out, the kind words, entertaining you.
I do it because I respected your late mother; she loved you; she would want me to.
I do it because you were part of my life when your mother, among others, exemplified kindness;
       they all would want me to. As part of a valued larger family.
I wish you also valued that larger family. Then we could be friends. It could be our bond.
Valuing the wider world together could be our bond.
I'd like that!
But you seem to think our bond is the shared understanding of how wonderful you are. Not me,
       not the rest of us, wonderful. Only you.
From me to you—okay? I'm done with giving you chances.
Go jump in a lake.

NOVEMBER 24

...*And,* to a certain nother person: Having the last say, you know, doesn't mean you're right.
Do you even know what a conversation is?
A conversation is when you say something and I open-mindedly consider it. Then I comment and...
You open-mindedly consider what I say.
We go back and forth a bit, with embellishing facts and personal insights, enhancing the subject.
    It is *pleasant*—especially the part where I get to know you better.
(For you, that would be the part where you're getting to know *me* better.)
If you have a definite opinion on something I might not agree, and if I have a definite opinion, you might not agree. So what?
This isn't warfare, and just because you're a big powerful male *certainly* doesn't make you right.
Even if we *were* arguing and you were to "win" it wouldn't necessarily mean you are right.
    Often the person with the best arguing skills scores points and wins—even if they are wrong. So I refrain from doing that to you. (I could.)
Thanks so much for appreciating it.
Arguing isn't a conversation, anyway, and I personally don't enjoy doing it.
A *conversation* is where each person comes away with a better and enriched understanding of the other person, and a better and enriched perspective on life.

NOVEMBER 25

...At least you're not a hypocrite.
Guess I'm anxious and stressed-out and came down a bit hard on you yesterday.
You're not nearly as difficult as You-Know-Who, who will also be showing up at my house tomorrow.
Mr. Suave-Debonaire, who says everything "perfectly right" and does everything "perfectly right"—
Except Sincerity.
Which transforms all his carefully constructed "rightness" into lies.
Except I forget—how can I forget?—you're not listening. (I am only someone to humor.)
The kids will be listening, though, and they'll be paying special attention to Mr. You-Know-Who. Whom they should not trust.
So I do say this for you: When push comes to shove, you're trustworthy. And you're sincere.
Fortunately the kids know to not pay attention to Mr. Debonaire's wife. She's too obvious. A pain-in-the-ass, but obvious.
Maybe you'll want to click-in and listen to me for this part: *Your* wife, Sir, is a delight.
Then stay tuned and consider: Your treatment of her is disgraceful.

NOVEMBER 26

It's here. Thanksgiving Day. This All-American holiday where kinfolk of all generations, genders, religions and political affiliations gather together to feast. Sometimes they bring along friends—and friends of friends—to share in the family experience.
Providing a great opportunity for us grown-ups to demonstrate harmony and inclusiveness for the kids. To show them that everyone deserves respect, and that the job of hosts is to make guests feel welcome and comfortable. On this particular day of Thanksgiving —fingers crossed!—perhaps to also pull off drawing everyone together in conscious gratitude.
For some family members, Thanksgiving is an annual opportunity to lay back, off-guard, saying obnoxiously whatever they really think and behaving, unfiltered, how they really are, because "That's why family is so great. They have to accept you, whoever you are." And the children? If by observing such inconsiderate behavior, could they be learning that when older they, too, will be entitled to do and say whatever strikes their fancy? (Of course *not now*, but something to look forward to when it's "their turn"?)

It has been my experience that every young child who, having had it explained to them how a small behavior change on their part brightens the day of someone they trust—they do it. They also describe as "pretty" any woman who is caring, happy, understanding—regardless how unstylish or disfigured she may be. "Handsome" men have a bold, warm sense of humor, and strength of spirit.
The holiday of Thanksgiving? Perhaps the greatest opportunity it offers is for us older folk to be mindful of the youngest ones and learn something *from them*.

NOVEMBER 27

Gotta get outta here.
Had enough!
Enough of enough.
Especially enough thinking. Gears are stripping! *Emotions* stripping!
To impulsively throw caution to the wind! Sometimes it's best to just—
GO!

(The worst part of yesterday being when my spouse didn't back up my efforts. He kept *undoing* them! And why did he even invite Mr. You-Know-Who and his family?)

NOVEMBER 28

The wind has wings!
And feathers, too.
A rushing, maelstrom blur.
White bodies lifting webbed orange feet
Into the raucous whirr.
Then in the startling vacance—
Lo.
A single, looping feather.

NOVEMBER 29

My dad. He did get one important thing wrong, but he was a good sport, no one tried harder than he did, and here is one of the many things he got right: Pigs. He said there was nothing cuter than a litter of piglets.
He also loved rollicky verse.
So on your birthday today, Dad—remembering you!

The piglets snurt and snort about,
They nudge and shove with glee,
Enjoying smells, fresh water, food—
With full tenacity.
They get it!
Live is to live. Embrace. Indulge!
So self aware and twink.
So healthy, eager, trying things out—
Pushing life to the brink.
They get it.
In roly scrambles, squeally gambols,
Artless gumptions commence.
So pinky, helpless, fresh and new.
Assured bold innocence.

NOVEMBER 30

Let's say you're dead. (Not dead in a morbid, frightening way. In a rational, speculative way.—
   In fact, you might conclude this is your favorite verse of the year.) So—back to being dead—and let's say the dying part wasn't too bad, that is to say no pain ,and you felt your loved ones loving you. Nonetheless, a goner you are, and you find you still possess a will. A mind.
Perhaps you had hoped this would be the case (as we are presently postulating!)—but have you
   given much thought to what you *would do* if you found yourself in that situation?
There will probably be "a light"—an illumination of space off in the distance. For a long time I
   was afraid that going into that light could mean not being able to come back out. A trap. I now think this isn't true—which makes sense. To *not* go into the light would mean you are trapped. In this world.
It makes sense that you could come and go from the light as you please—if that's your will—
   which is today's topic:
Your will.

First, you must know what you want—so why not want something good?
If you are scientifically minded and had always fantasized about exploring strange new worlds,
   then "will" yourself there by imagining really being in a new "somewhere". Then you might find yourself there! Perhaps off exploring caverns, if you love caverns. (Or for others, how about a stint admiring piglets...)

Keeping your thoughts clear and unfettered.
Apparently there's glory and utmost satisfaction in the light. Regardless of who you are or what
   you've done here on earth. Imagine such glory for yourself—enter on into the light—

And know the glory!
It will feel right, because it *IS* right.

If you are artistically minded, you could try envisioning configurations of artistic, structural, or architectural merit. Whatever it is you enjoy! And *endlessly*—if you so decide.
Part of your heart may well still lie here on earth, in this realm, in the lives of people you love and remain concerned about. If so, "will" a connection with them. Watch over them.— Although you may find they have wills of their own, and confusions, obstructing a connection.
—Or other energies or conduits might interfere with connections.
Keep figuring it out—but don't expect to learn in the same manner that your mind grew in this physical world, as it interacted with the physical. So if you value knowledge and information, this is the best time to use your brain to keep acquiring knowledge and information. You won't be able to imagine well if you are not aware of the possibilities.
—And it will have helped to have not died in a state of torment, mental chaos, or physical pain. If you did, then you will have to deal with that also, while adjusting to your new state of being.

What, you may wonder, about the "time" element? So many ways to speculate regarding time!
Additionally, although much may not seem possible, there shouldn't be any reason why you can't pick-and-choose which aspects of yourself to make available to those who are still alive. (Which I shall do in my parting blessing to you.)

Remember!—If you find you are no longer connected with your body, to keep a clear, calm presence. Know what you want. If it helps, remember to focus on a single calm thing or single calm person you love, until you get your bearings.

DECEMBER

DECEMBER 1

Right now what I'm imagining is telling off several more people. Sorry to say, they are big strong men—who revel in being big and strong. They overdo it.

They "rough it" up to Alaska each summer then return to tell the tales (oh, the tales they tell!) of their survival skills (exemplary!) and bragging about their encounters with grizzly bears.

The grizzly bear part is where to draw the line. Up until then a little, *eh*, possible embellishment of survival skills—no problem. Somewhat stimulating, actually—the other ladies present are finding it so—*but stop there!* Do not hurt the bears if you don't have to!—and certainly *do not lure* them into being hurt.

Now *FOR SURE* stop. But no. Now "us ladies" are supposed to look up to you for being braver than we are. (Why can't you be satisfied with your great outdoorsman skills?) The bravery part—since you bring it up—*let me tell you about bravery:*

You think grizzly bears are bad? I would rather be up against a mindless brute grizzly bear than up against a vengeful, cunning, predatory male human. Not only can they muscularly overpower and maim (as can bears), but while it's happening the thought of being ravaged—and possibly killed!—by someone *we want to like*—with *premeditation* to harm us—and *intent* to make it personal—

Can you imagine *THAT!?* Every time we find ourselves alone on an empty street or unintentionally trapped or lured in by one—there we are confronting a "worse than a grizzly bear"—but the alternative is to stay secluded and not engage in living, in life. So we do go places and we do engage—but can you see the risks women take each time we do? Everyday women, in everyday life. *How's that for bravery?*

(The solution, of course, being to restrict the freedom of those select males. Or for them to decide on their own that they don't want to be despicable and to "solve themselves.")

If you want to be brave, you over-the-top male adventurers, I can tell you how to be brave: To be truly brave, try facing unpleasant facts. Something that, if true, could undermine your sense of self and your validity as a person. Something deep in your childhood—perhaps since infancy—that you have built loyalties and a life upon. If you do, maybe your life *won't* come crashing down—but maybe it will. To take *that kind of a chance,* in order to be a fair and just person.
I will admire your bravery then.

DECEMBER 2

To the woman who had an affair with my husband: *How dare you?* On multiple counts.
You knew us and knew we were married. How dare you go around passing yourself off as such a nice person who was just being his friend. And for his part? He was just being your friend?
Did you miss the lesson—way back in elementary school—on what friendship is?
And now that my ex has dumped you too, how dare you have the nerve to walk up to me, all nicey-nice, pretending to be *my* friend?
While you're enthralled in your syrupy monologue, let me process this—with mounting disgust for you. While I'm still processing, though, you have now become flagrantly angry—*at me??*—because I'm not following along with you and sympathizing with how disappointed and hurt he caused you to be? Poor, mistreated you.
Okay. Got my thoughts together. Let me remind you of something. Remember back when your husband divorced you? Do you recall the barrage of words you used to describe the woman he'd cheated on you with? Choice words indeed, they were.
Before I get a chance to calmly and succinctly relate this, however, my date has pulled me back. He pulled *ME* back. *YOU* were the one who had approached me! He's not letting me stand my ground!
So here is my second shot at getting this out:
"Please bring to mind every foul expletive you heaped upon your ex's mistress. That is your opinion of women who do things like that. Then take a hard, long, honest look in a mirror. THAT. IS. YOU."

DECEMBER 3

A world without faith. Can you picture such a world?
A world with no one taking leaps of faith beyond what they know-to-be-true, to what they believe must-be-true.
No one taking chances on being someone's friend, or loving someone, or engaging in *anything* of value—because of the hurt that ensues when they get it wrong.
What kind of a world would it be?

DECEMBER 4

When suffering because of the unjust decision of another, how to handle it?
This happens in measures great or small throughout everyone's life. Off-and-on being a victim is part of life!
Some situations may require an instantaneous reaction. Other times you might have the luxury of being able to settle and organize your thoughts before responding—or to have had your thoughts organized beforehand, as per the motto "always be prepared." Although—
Off-and-on being blindsided is also part of life.
Would you feel alone in handling the situation, or would you feel supported? By friends? By family? By having trust that organizations or the legal system have your back?

Next, pretend you are not the victim of an unjust decision, but a bystander of a victim.
As a bystander, the *minimum* that can be done is to acknowledge, for the person who is hurting, that, yes, an injustice was done and no, they did not deserve it. (You can manage that much?)
That's likely all you need do, and they can take it from there!

Back to you as the one wronged. Consider and bring to mind a situation in which you had been wronged. The question: Are you blaming others, perhaps casting wildly about to place blame anywhere other than on yourself?
Perhaps doing this *simultaneously* with trying to figure out what might have been your part in the misfortune?—
Or perhaps blaming *only yourself?* Wracking your brain to *not* think ill of whoever mistreated you, giving them every benefit of every doubt.
A concern, that last possibility. Which is where—

Bystanders (back to you as a bystander!) come in. You may have to go beyond simply acknowledging the victim's victimhood, to *over-acknowledging it*. Making too big of a deal of how they didn't deserve the treatment!—and all the things wrong with the offender! When the victim is going overboard blaming themself. To balance out their conflict. Until—

The victim is able to stabilize, balancing it out themself.
Which brings us full circle back to the starting point. Once you've stabilized after having suffered an injustice—then you get to be the person you want to be:
Forgiving? Vengeful?
Seeking continued support and companionship with those who helped you?
Paying their support forward by helping others?
Dumping those who abandoned you or kicked you when you were down?
Dumping those who tried to add to your confusion for their own gain? Including, inciting you to make mistakes.
Or perhaps, as some do, to bury the incidents and forget they ever happened.

DECEMBER 5

Deliberately stomping footprints in the snow says...
You've been here!
Would be nice if all the snow hereabouts was unblemished and pristine, a blank slate for your stomps, but it's not. Although—*perhaps*—it might be...
Even better?
Look—
Rabbit tracks. A bunny has been here, too! *That* makes the snow better.
And over there, under the trees—have deer passed through here as well? Who cares if there's a little mud mixed in with it all? Streaks and splots of mud here and there make the scene more authentic!
And hopping birds? Yes-yes, at the water's edge—there had been a profusion of hopping birds!
This gets better and better! And as such...
Stomp! Stomp! Stomp! Stomp! Stomp!
Why not add to the spirit of the thing?
We are *all* part of this frozen, snow-encrusted juncture—
Rabbits, deer, birds—*all of nature!*—and let it be known that included in the thrill of the season is... *You,* and the traces *You* are leaving. *YOU* are decisively included!
STOMP!—Yes!

DECEMBER 6

There it is! Quick! The fluffiest, most ebullient sphere you have ever seen! How can it not be
      magical?
Looks ever-so-soft—but could that be a trick of the eye? Vibrating faster than one can blink.
      Than one can think!
Call it a vibratey-with-vim-cycle.
(Not thinking here...)
Yet pleasantly solemn—as a hymn.
A blurry soft shimmy-ing hymn-sical.
A shimmy-sical that twitchingly settles into...

Real life...
Feathers and beak
And huff.
Is this a let down?—or could its reality be *better* than magic?
Behold you here (*chirpy drum roll...*)—
The whimsical!

DECEMBER 7

Arctic fox, arctic fox, white as snow.
Arctic fox, arctic fox, where did you go?
I am here.
Arctic lemming, down below,
Sheltered beneath three feet of snow.
Are you safe?

He can sense you—the smart fox.
He leaps, he plunges! to your spot.

Did he nab you? Oh, poor lemming.
Did he miss? Poor hungry fox.

Who remains in the arctic snow?
In the vast, white frozen tundra.

I am here.
(But who??)

DECEMBER 8

Hello? *Knock-knock-knock.*
Hey, Buffalo, anybody home? Under all that curly, swirly hair. Which is
Under all the swirly, curly wind and snow—
And ice.
Frozen, icicle hair.
Knock-knock-knock. You alive in there?
Yes! A swirly-curly breath!
Buffalo is—in!
(...*Grummpha.*)

DECEMBER 9

Boney, stoney, cold hunger.
Boney.
Stoney.
Cold.
An unfilled capacity.
An unfilled need.
How best to proceed?
How intense the deprivation?
A boney, stoney, cold outlook
When one feels desperation.

DECEMBER 10

It can be said that desperation is the root of all evil.
Anger may precede desperation, but anger also precedes positive change.
It depends on why one is angry—and then on what one does about it.
To despair is to not see or believe there is a way out of direness, suffering, pain.
Perhaps because there is no way out.
Then friends and well-wishers can do what they can to help them cope.
But desperation fueled by anger—a self-righteous, locked-in anger—is what creates...
Evil.

DECEMBER 11

It's a cookie day!
Time to roll up your sleeves, gather the ingredients together—and let's get these rollin' pins rollin'. (*smiley face*)

You'll need:
    1/2 cup sugar
    1/2 cup butter (one cube, room temperature)
    2 eggs
    2-1/2 - 3 cups flour
    2 teaspoons baking powder
    1 teaspoon vanilla

Cream the butter and sugar together (a fork can work for that). Beat in the remaining ingredients, adding just enough flour for smooth, easy rolling. Knead it a bit to see, then form into two balls. Cover them in wrap and chill in the refrigerator for at least two hours.

While they're chilling, preheat oven to 350°, and lightly butter a cookie sheet.
For the icing gather together:

    3 cups powdered sugar
    2/3 cup lemon juice (you probably won't need it all) or water
    Food coloring
    Assorted nuts, raisins, candies, sprinkles

Time to roll! Roll out the dough to about 1/4" thick on a lightly floured surface, patting lightly with flour as you go so the dough doesn't stick to the rolling pin. Then cut with cookie cutters into your desired shapes. (Geometric shapes? Holiday shapes? Animals?) For circles, an inverted drinking glass works well as a cutter.

Bake 7-10 minutes, until edges are just slightly brown. (The browner you let them become, the crispier the cookies will be—and oh, so buttery!—until—*oops*—watch out or they'll burn.) Once removed from the oven, let them "set" on the cookie sheet for several minutes, then remove to a cooling rack to finish cooling.

For the icing, keep stirring lemon juice into the powdered sugar until spreadable. If you make it too thin by mistake, have extra powdered sugar at hand to add to thicken it back up. Divide into small bowls for each color—just a drop or two of food color per bowl is usually enough.

Now the grand finale! Ice and sprinkle and decorate your cookies to your heart's content. Imagining which cookie will be for which select person! And don't forget some… smiley faces!

DECEMBER 12

Every adult wants to be in charge of their own life.
To know how to make the best decisions, solve their life problems, know whom to trust.
Those raised in protective bubbles struggle to achieve this state. If they ever do.
Innocents struggling to achieve selfhood in a non-innocent world.
Let us help them!
Let us ease them safely out from their state of vulnerability. From being easily manipulated by those who use them for their own ends. From not learning how to work constructively through their frustrations and anger. And worst of all (from their point of view) from being unable to protect and make the best decisions regarding those they love.
Let those of us who idealize adult innocence, cease and desist! doing so.

DECEMBER 13

As a postulation, let's say it's possible for someone to be a "perfect human being." That the ideal exists, and that it is achievable.

Which raises the question: Who is to say what the "ideal" human is? In the past, some have claimed that perfection is to never make a mistake (and that they—how coincidental!—qualify as perfect under this definition). Others have held that maintaining someone in a perpetual state of innocence establishes their perfection—which would mean whatever that person spontaneously does and says is "pure" and unassailable.

Are you seeing any unreasonableness here?—or maybe a definite "no"?

Hence—

Definitions have arisen that include making mistakes and growth into account. Such as: "A perfect person is one who always does the best they can."

A-hem. Let's examine that. Imagine someone going through life doing the best they can, and fancying themself "perfect" because of it. A living embodiment of humanity's ideal—mistakes and all—because they make a point to do *some* learning from the mistakes...

And let's say—to your eye and to mine—they are doing abysmally poorly, causing grave and avoidable damage. Yet there they are, all smug and swaggery, believing they're just fine, thank you.

...Whereas others who cause damage get all racked-up about it. Aware they had a part in causing it (thus, not an ideal person!) and *most importantly* aware when they choose to not address the damage—and are racked *about that*, in addition. They wish they were a better person. But get sidelined—lost—in addressing more immediate concerns.

...As such, desiring to address the damage, it can be said they are putting their "best self" on hold. They have an awareness of a "best self" somewhere inside them, and when opportunities arise to become that improved self, let's say they jump at the chance. Keeping a continual lookout for such possibilities.

Not complacent.

Fundamental self-doubt. Stuck in a place in life where there are some sacrifices they are simply unwilling to make—and in the gap between that and their desire for atoning—

Great accomplishments can be achieved.

As an example, let's dissect Thomas Jefferson. (Always bracing to dissect and examine our flawed Mr. U.S.A.) Thomas Jefferson believed in equality for all humans—in principle—but there were real-life actions he couldn't bring himself to do. Given the "deals in life" he had accepted when he was growing up, and the prices he'd paid and the loyalties he'd established—he felt freeing his slaves would be unfair to himself. Including negatively impacting his ability to function.

We will speculate that instead, he did what he could to clear a path for future generations to treat people fairly. In compensation for his inadequacy. The shining light he left for us, that "all men are created equal," was of monumental import not only to the U.S.A. but to the entire world—yet it was a gift he might not have bothered bestowing, and so decidedly, had he not had a nagging awareness of his hypocrisy and felt compelled to do *something*.

The world lost out on one more plantation owner setting a good example by conscientiously liberating his slaves, but gained something more lasting and far-reaching.

(Assuming Jefferson had that awareness—at least in the back of his mind—of his shortcomings, and was uneasy—at least in the back of his mind—of the justifications and excuses he kept coming up with. If not him, though, there are other examples of the gap between unwillingness and atoning.)

Those who go through life "on hold" can accomplish wonders. They continually wish they could do more than follow the established path, and look for opportunities others aren't open to seeing—and seize them.

They realize they're flawed, and how they would describe what constructive actions they take is that they're trying to make up for prior ignorance, and for the times luck failed them when they took reasonable chances, and for when luck smiled on them when they were reckless but did not smile on others equally reckless, and for wanting to up the overall odds of good things happening in the world.

Those who feel they are fine-just-the-way-they-are, especially if backed by many commendable and hailed accomplishments, can stagnate—even strangulate—us.

In conclusion: It can be said that those who deep-down-implicitly *know* they are not perfect are the perfect ones. The human ideal. Except it is impossible for them to know they are (or they would not be). It is only others who can spot them out.

DECEMBER 14

Away off yonder—an island of bodies clustered densely together for warmth levitates above a wide horizontal pond.
The levitating island stretches nearly the width of the pond it covers, and is lumpy-bumpy with the bodies,
With both the wide pond and island above it paralleling a distant, low mountain range. Which is slightly bumpy. A long horizontal slash of dim mountains.
Between the suspended island and pond below, visually linking them, are a verticality of spindly legs.

The scene bespeaks a chilled evening quietude, punctuated with wisps of piercing wind, aggressively rippling the sheen of the pond
And weaving forcefully through the forest of thin legs.
Accumulations of secrets—adamantly whipping through the legs.
Secrets of distances and reflections.
Secrets of whimsy.
Secrets of endurance.

DECEMBER 15

Here's a team for the brave—no faint of heart.
Team Mother Earth.
You are welcome to join—okay if you don't—but if you do, it takes workouts and dedication.
The deeper you engage, the deeper your sense of camaraderie and belonging.
The goal? To optimize the experiences and harmony of life on Earth.
To get in shape? Acquire information and keep your brain well-tuned with critical thinking skills, and up-to-speed with healthy eating habits.
The playbook? To glory in science! All sciences. Supporting and contributing to discoveries.
To creatively assimilate and share the discoveries.
The enemy? Chaos.

Two—Four—Six—Eight—
Who do we appreciate?
Ma-Ma! Ma-Ma Earth!

What is victory?
To triumph over chaos.

DECEMBER 16

No one asked to be born. No person—no creature—no being. Yet here we are!
None are to be blamed for existing.
Perhaps it would be a kindness—perhaps even *a right*—for each human to be made welcome.
To grant each dignity. So they can feel right within themselves. So they don't have to struggle
    to feel validated. (As if, maybe, they *don't deserve* to exist.)
So then the question: What would a basic welcome entail? For babies—
That their physical needs be met? Food, clothing, shelter—medical care?
That each feel loved by the person taking care of them?
That they are provided a basic education and adequate opportunities for personal growth?
A healthy world to live in—clean air, fresh water, a balance of human and animal populations
    within a balanced and rich environment?

What about an adult's basic rights?
Are you familiar with the *Universal Declaration of Human Rights?* It's an extraordinary
    document! It was drawn up in 1948 by the United Nations General Assembly, and signed
    by all 193 member states. Please read it—all 30 articles, most self-explanatory, but I
    would draw your attention to Article 22 regarding the right to social security.
    Interpretations may vary, but hopefully this means a person's right to just laze around if
    they so decide, unpressured, without stigma.—
A small, safe, *extremely basic* space guaranteed for each person, with an *extremely basic* income
    —enough to supply themselves with *basic* needs only. If they want more than that, then
    they can join the larger society by getting a job and earning more.
(Could not the world's economic system—which liberally spends more money elsewhere—
    shuffle its ratios and spring for this smaller expense?)

DECEMBER 17

No one's looking! Making sure my nappy won't slip down this time...
Double checking on the nappy...
Looking back. Still no Mom, no Dad.
Carefully... Oh so silently and carefully... Opening—the—doooor...
Jay-Jay has escaped!

Quickly, out past the patio. Down into the lower yard! Carefully around the big shadows—the big, um, hose-wrappy thingy... Everything is so, so DARK—so cold—so black—so... DIFFERENT. This is a different world! This is...
Oh! My! God!

Jay-Jay has looked up. White pin-pricked stars as he has never seen stars before. Smattered thickly across a heavens—as he has never seen nor could have imagined a heavens to be! Stars smattered as far and wide and deep as... eternity! The vastness and inexplicability of eternity, and... it... is... inside him! He feels it. He knows it! The depth of the heavens and all its stars belong to him—and ARE HIM.
A small human child, mindlessly holding tight to his slipping nappy—
Gobsmacked!

Jay-Jay reaches up to grasp his twinkling stars—reaching, reaching—grasping, grasping.

DECEMBER 18

There are two sides to empathy.
One is the positive side we hear so much about, where one feels everyone else's pain-emotions-joys, and how that gives rise to more understanding in the world.
But there is also the "creepy" side of empathy. As a matter of personal privacy, maybe someone doesn't want you getting inside their skin, privy to their secret feelings, sensitivities and vulnerabilities. Especially if the person "sensing you" is an enemy!—who would use the information against you.—
But also regarding friends, one needs barriers. A way to maintain individuality without "blending into" everyone else—until all of humanity becomes one big communal blob of emotions.
Turns out there is a way to keep this from happening—although it gives one pause.
To form a firm barrier of self, one needs to work on solidifying themself as an individual—with unique experiences, heart-felt interests and loves, their own plans, personalized desires, knowing who they are... Then as the more solid they become, the more encased and impervious to merging with others.
...Which positions them to better understand and empathize with all the other solidly encased individuals!
And as such—the more defined and solid they are, the more there is for others to empathize with

The greater the abundance of firm individualities, the more empathy there can be, linking one and all. Not an amorphous mishy-mush of all beings, trespassing all over one another, but a composite of many distinct souls forming up into something...
Grand?

DECEMBER 19

The mystery deepens.

What mystery? It can be said there are as many mysteries as there are points of view. There is the basic mystery of existence, there is...

Yes, throw those in too. The mystery deepens...

I wasn't through...

They *all* deepen. All the mysteries deepen.

Why would they all deepen? What about bringing them to light and unraveling them in order to understand them? What about SCIENCE? Isn't science supposed to keep on sorting everything out until all the mysteries lessen?

There is the mystery of that, too.

(Humph.) You mean the ol' "the more we know the more we know we don't know"? That whenever one mystery is solved, more mysteries become apparent?

You don't experience wonder in that?

I want to know what you're talking about.

I'm talking about the possibility of alternate realities.

Can't science solve that?

Our science is within our reality. We experience everything through *our* senses, *our* intellect, *our* accumulations of knowledge and understanding. Which expands our reality, and whenever we make decisions based on it (exercising our free will). But which, when seen in the context of different realities also existing, might not be taking something vital into account.

To say that would be speculating with OUR intellect.

Exactly. As such... The mystery deepens.

DECEMBER 20

Can an answer to a question be that there is no answer? Whether you say "yes" or "no"—
We're talking about there being a question.
To which an answer might not exist.
Which itself would be an answer, because allowing there is no answer is nonetheless *an answer*.
     A placeholder answer. (In the manner that 0 is a number.)
Which means "no answer" is an answer.
To have never formulated a question to begin with is a nothingness. To have never wondered
     about something—to have never experienced wonder—
Is a nothingness.

DECEMBER 21

Here's to men! Adult male humans.
As individuals you've been getting a bum rap.
As a group, much of the world is comprised of male-dominated sexist patriarchies.
But each little boy has no ownership in that.
Sweet, kind little boys who adore their mothers and (at heart) adore their sisters—and *all women*.
    And who want to do right by them. Wanting them to be happy!
To rewind (one more time) into world history here. The part where in many of our ancestral civilizations there wasn't much in the way of a middle class. When men were either wealthy or living in poverty—abject poverty, and many didn't have a choice but to labor long hours in subservient, harsh conditions. Sometimes dehumanizing conditions. The gentle, kind men among them sorrowful that their women (whom they liked) were in on the suffering.
Meanwhile... The gentle, kind men who were wealthy must have known of the prevalent injustices and amorality of their non-gentle peers. They would have wanted to keep their women (whom they liked—remember we're talking about the ones who like women)—they would have wanted to keep their womenfolk from having to compromise their integrity and purity (as they were having to do, in order to maintain their wealth). It was necessary for them to be impure and play dirty at times, thus maintaining institutional injustices—or else they would lose their status, and their women and children would go down with them. Be reduced to poverty. (Plus, along with that, they might have been imagining how wonderful it must feel "being pure" and that their women were grateful for being kept that way, but unless the women were worldly they would not have had the wherewithal to appreciate it. What they would have thought was that men were inherently inferior and women inherently superior, and their men were simply paying them due tribute.)

The men in the upper classes who *were* sexist, however—who resented women and wanted to keep them "in their place"—*those* men ran the show. It was hard for a solitary nice guy to break their hold on that!

Enter—*finally!*—an age with the rise of middle classes, where the two extremes of wealth and poverty are all mixing in together.

So that now (*this is such a good part!*) men who like women are increasingly able to break the male-supremacy hold of millennium.

So! Here's to Men! To each *individual* man who is presently living a life that engages in doing that. To modern-day kind, gentle men who stand up to die-hard sexism—to discrimination against *any* gender. Who are doing what they can to break down sexist institutions.

...And to *everyone*, each and all, who is doing what they can to break down racist institutions—and ALL institutions that exploit and abuse others.

DECEMBER 22

This one's for you, Donna. Older sister extraordinaire—when it counted most. When we were young.
Three-and-a-half years apart doesn't seem much of an age difference now, but while growing up that's a large age gap. It was large enough for me to look up to you as a protector—a role you filled well enough—and a nurturer—*ta da!* there you were, acknowledging me! And as an awesome, tender, dynamite personality.
You were also someone who had the gift of insight into character (which I still have to work for) and the aura of wisdom that comes with that talent. Solidness. Common sense. (Mingled with your spright, earthy sense of humor...) And after initial restraint when confronted with a problem, then boldness, when initiative was called for. Leadership qualities.
Seeing how you were being treated for your initiative and not being able to help both angered and defeated me. I was not worthy of you. I was fearful, holding back—a coward—knowing I couldn't pull it off and would make everything worse—although I (somehow) simultaneously assumed you could handle the problems by yourself. You could handle anything!
Until you couldn't.
What I would like you to know now, that perhaps you didn't know then, is that I can recall few incidents when I wasn't on your side. You were fundamentally the one in the right!
I thought you were brave for standing up for your causes, for those in your care, and for your own personal rights.
Whereas I wasn't brave.
Until I was.
But by then it was too late for you.

DECEMBER 23

To hold onto the ideal. The *ultimate ideal*. That of the goodness and rightness of existence.
Is it an ideal you claim?
Yet everyday life forces us to focus on what is immediately in front of us. On whatever situations must presently be dealt with.
Quotidian life.
It can be easy to lose sight of ideals—or to have difficulty integrating them into the situation at hand.
Such fumbling and ineptitudes can become engrained patterns of behavior. Patterns accepted by our social networks, our families, our cultures. Patterns that can be hard to break!
And when one gets lost in anger, that for sure blocks their connection with higher ideals.
But the ideal of goodness and rightness *does* exist—even when not readily visible—and by having faith in that, with our choices we have the freedom—and the honor—to turn aspects of the ideal into reality.

DECEMBER 24

Peace.
Both overrated and underrated.
Peace.
"Peace be with you."—*Peace on Earth!*—
All of us living together in harmony. Great! ...Right?
But what kind of harmony?
The mere absence of conflict makes for neither a satisfying nor a lasting peace. That kind of
        harmony is stifling. Boring.
An interesting harmony then? Full of surprises, challenges, personal satisfactions...
Yes? (...Yes!)
A peace and harmony among cultures and individuals that keeps one on one's toes—addressing
        new situations with freshness, and each individual lighting up with new personalized
        happiness...
Or thrashing about with new personalized unhappiness, when one gets it wrong.
The right, within specified contexts, to take chances and get it wrong?

One thing we know for sure: The world is ever-changing.
With each new sunrise... with each new technological development... with each new birth...
        with *your* birth... the world will never be the same. Your birth alone has kept the world
        interesting!
And with the birth of each and all of the other new people!
Finding ways to adjust to the multiplicity of changes remains, ever, the challenge.

Generations that preceded us have left us their world, as is—we had no choice about what we got
        —but we have a big choice about how we maintain our world and what we pass along to
        those who will come after us. Who will in their turn pass it on.

Will the ones newly in charge take the responsibility of maintenance seriously? Will they appreciate and build upon what is good? Might they opt for indiscriminately tearing down what doesn't serve their immediate purposes?
How do *we* fare on those counts?

Will future generations be able to keep those who are bent on destruction from rising to positions of power? Will they be able to distinguish between what is mortally dangerous and what is merely taking a reasonable chance or two? (Being rash.)

To what extent will they take into account the lessons their parents learned, especially as regards war?

To what extent did *you* learn from the long line of ancestors preceding you, regarding conflict and war?

No generation can bequeath a lasting peace to succeeding generations. Each new generation is on their own to make the most of whatever peace they inherit—using their own judgment and making their own choices. It is an ever-changing, ongoing process. Peace can not be locked in!
But if we care about those in the upcoming generation, the best we can do is pass on a healthy world to them.
To up the odds of them establishing their own
Peace.

DECEMBER 25

Above the deep and dreamless sleep...
Listen. The night wind is saying something to a little lamb. Then—

Yonder breaks a new and glorious morn!
The hopes and fears of all the years are met.
An everlasting light.
Relief!

Joy to the world!
The soul feels its worth!
Celebration!

Caroling, caroling, through the snow,
Christmas bells are ringing.
Happiness!

Peace.
Goodwill henceforth from Heav'n to men begin and never cease...
Umm... Um. Maybe claiming this is going too far?
And as if *everyone* had been in a deep and dreamless sleep...

But look up! Is the sky not imbued with
A song, a song, high above the trees, with a voice as big as the sea.

Let Heaven and Nature sing! Let Heaven and Nature sing! Let Heav-en—let Heav-en—and
    Nature sing.

DECEMBER 26

Let's say you're bursting with joy and love, and in this euphoria of goodwill and generosity toward all humankind you wish, for everyone, that they could feel as you do.
Have you ever experienced and tried sharing that euphoric feeling?
If so, how did that work for you? And for those with whom you attempted to share it?
Consider Elizabeth's words to her sister Jane in *Pride and Prejudice*. Jane had careened from happiness to *acute* anxiety to despair to—acute relief! Joy! And wished her dear sister Elizabeth to experience the same joy in her life. But Lizzy replied,
"I never could be so happy as you. Till I have your disposition, your goodness, I never can have your happiness. No, no, let me shift for myself…"
Lizzy knew that what worked for Jane wouldn't apply to her. They were different people, in different situations. *But then—*
It turned out Lizzy did find a joyous path. But not because of anything Jane said or did.—
At least not directly. Do you think Jane's intentions and "prayers" might have had some effect?
Then ask yourself, what if "euphoric Jane," in attempting to impose her own brand of happiness on Lizzy by means that would have worked *for her*, might have had the opposite effect on Lizzy? If Jane had persisted, might she have stood in her sister's way, precluding her from experiencing her own intense joy?

DECEMBER 27

A day of frost, crystals and icicles is a day of
Prisms.
A lively cinerama of sharp angles, multi-facetness, refractions of light:
Refracted, minute winking rainbows.
Refracted, fragmented ways of looking at everything—
Of looking *amongst* everything.
Interactive pinpoint focuses.
Myriad merging, reflecting.
Fleeting clarity—clouding smoothly away
Into darkened, freezing mist.
—Shifting sharply back into focus!
Happening within a white panorama of smooth, far snow.
This serene day of stillness—*alive! splintering brightly!*
With prismatics.

DECEMBER 28

How can an elderly person be "cute"? I mean, isn't that dismissive?
Somehow by now I had thought—hoped—to have accumulated a lifetime of stately respect.
Alas. If I get a new haircut, it's usually "Oh, how cute!" A new hat?—(am partial to hats)—it's "Oh, you look so cute in that hat!" So it goes.
Isn't cuteness a designation for children?—for the young?
As a child, however, I wasn't considered cute—at least not in the eyes of my community or family. Fell short of their mark of being "sweet" and "cooperative."
Had not felt young then.
I feel young now.
It seems most people start out feeling young, decide they like it, then do what they can to hang onto the feeling. Some hang on to it by stunting their flow of growing up—even when doing so does not serve them well. Having felt young when they *were* young was a gift given to them by the skill of others.
Perhaps they would be better off recognizing and being grateful for having been given that gift. For having spent their youngest years feeling good about themselves!
For me, much of my adulthood has involved learning how to feel young for the first time, and replicating, for myself, the trust and security of it. (Then passing that on to others.)

We all go back and revisit parts of our lives to some extent, then forward again—mixing up the order of living, and refreshing ourselves in the process.
May the order of living that you choose for yourself be of the pattern and style that work best for you!
(My cumulative blessing to you tomorrow...)

DECEMBER 29

As time passes—as it will—and my mortality has come to an end—as it will—
Let me be a whisper. A kind word whispered to you when you could use a kind word.
Let me be a kiss. A butterfly kiss, as light on your forehead as the brush of a butterfly wing, but with depth of understanding.
Although for everyone other than my family and personal friends, it will not be the soft kiss and kind sympathy of an old lady. It is from the little girl.
Because I was a kind little girl who loved and never (knowingly) harmed animals, and who was true to my friends. Childhood friends who knew I was thoughtful and sensitive, which meant *everything* to me. It was others who marked me as unwanted and cruel.
So in my farewell blessing, if you are to accept it, please know the favor is on me, to counter that deep marking. I would like that. As reinforced validation of myself that I had hoped, so long ago, to one day come true. And to also serve as validation for you.—
Passing along to you what my childhood friends once gave to me.
For I am planning to mostly stay around in the afterlife and let my child aspects be available.
My adult sensibilities, you find in these pages. My blessing:
Let the whisper, and soft kiss, and light touch on your forearm of this true and faithful child— *your friend*—be there for you.

DECEMBER 30

We live within a wonderment
Of creatures great and small,
     With stars above
     And all each loves—
Full worthy, short and tall.
Of dignity. For all.

We live within a richness
Where traps lie and dreams call.
     Where peace upends
     And fate descends
In struggles and windfalls.

We had no choice, each finds ourself
Here in life's wild enthrall.
     Each trapped, but free,
     In sympathy
With all who soar and crawl.
To bow within the squall

In dignity—
For all.

DECEMBER 31

The lemming had a narrow escape!
It pops its head up out of the collapsed snow.
Looks right, left, high, afar—sniffing in deep.
No arctic fox.
So much for peacefully trying to make it through Winter!
And just look at my carefully burrowed home!
But...
I'm still here.
And somewhere...
Foxes are still here.
And somewhere, somehow...
We are all still here.
Flipping back down now!
An it-is-what-it-is flick of its stubby little tail.

www.ingramcontent.com/pod-product-compliance
Lightning Source LLC
Chambersburg PA
CBHW060417300426
44111CB00018B/2879